UNKNOWN MASTER WITHIN

notionpress.com

Unknown Master Within

Santhosh Sukumaran

notionpress.com

Notion Press

5 Muthu Kalathy Street, Triplicane,

Chennai - 600 005

First Published by Notion Press 2014

ISBN: 978-93-83808-55-7

Unknown Master Within

We all know what fate and time are. Different people have different opinions on this; let me explain according to my knowledge, these two are different in many ways. We have heard people saying "It's all your fate." At times, when something goes wrong in some situations, they tend to say "It's all my fate," putting the blame on fate for our mistake for no reason, is that right? Fate is what we created, a word or an excuse to escape from our own mistakes, it does not happen automatically, never happens at all. It is natural that humans make mistakes because they do not happen automatically, it just happens. Fate never decides our life, we do. Let me come to time, when I say time it's totally automatic; today's life is totally involved with time, rather to blame on fate. We are scheduled in our day to day life accordingly. As days go on even time moves on, time is involved rather than fate in our lives; we plan our lives according to time, not by fate, the more you spend, your life is based on time not fate, I hope I am clear on this. Time takes us to good and bad aspects, when we move on with our life, on some occasions time decides what is best for us, time decides situations, according to situations we learn things and we react accordingly. Happiness and sadness can be judged through time, you may have come across situations in life where you might be happy or just the opposite of it. Years have passed very fast, but still people blame it on fate, it's the new generation where people don't have time to realize their mistake, to be reminded either about fate or time. But still there are people out there who happen to believe in all these things. The fact is, we people have been brought up believing in all these factors regarding fate and time, but when it comes to life it's only your life involved, not fate or time, people saw these factors as an excuse in life, so they started blaming in order to survive in life, people believed in fate and time when life seemed to be difficult. I too believed in these factors in the beginning until and unless I figured it out, maybe the society we are into is made of these kind of attitudes which cannot be changed, fate is what God decides at the time of our birth, but time is what we decide when life moves on, the experiences that I am going to share are all about my life, which involves these factors which I don't believe in. These factors made me realize the real me in my life, when one fine day I understood these factors never follow us, we follow it. Apart from these two factors there is another factor which follows your entire life, from generation to generation, young to old, all living beings in this world. Can you guess what is it all about? Yes, that's the right answer, you guessed it well. t's nothing else but love. Love is God, love is life, without love there is no life, from the time of your birth till the time of your death you're into this love through parents, friends, teachers, girlfriends and boyfriends, life partner, siblings, your kids, it has no ending it goes on. Let's start to encounter the experience of my life which turned out to be a bliss, let me not keep you bored by dragging out this topic and soon get into the journey of love.

My name is Santhosh Sukumaran. The first name Santhosh means happy all the time, some don't get it.

There is a word called "Santhosham" in Tamil which exactly means happiness all the time. When I was a little kid my mother used to tell me that my grandfather named me so, she used to tell me I never stopped smiling when I was a baby, so he named me so by looking at my smile. How sweet of him to name me like that. I am reminded about people telling me on occasions that happiness can be judged by the way you smile. I don't know how far that is true, but I know a smile can change an angry man to be calm one, definitely everyone does agree on this. There are incidents in my life which I am about to share that would have happened to others as well in their lives at some point.

I would not say this book is going to turn your life upside down, but there are some points which can be observed at some point of my life which you would have forgot to look into. It's all up to an individual's opinion whether to follow it or not. Maybe the experiences which I had in my life may sound stupid, may seem dramatically visualized, as I said it's all up to an individual to believe it or not.

I am thirty two years old, I was born in the month of March, my mother used to tell I was born the day before Shivaratri, Shivaratri is an Indian festival celebrated every year in the name of Hindu Lord Shiva, you may think, why did I mention this? Nothing special, just wanted to. I am from a middle class family a family of four including my younger brother. I was born in Kerala, the state we call "God's Own Country" due to the beauty of greenery it possesses. Tourists mostly visit here due to the nature and climatic conditions, and I have heard most of them saying that God lives in here in the form of nature. I spent most of my life in Tamilnadu, which is another state in India, especially my academic years. As I mentioned that my name has a meaning which says 'happiness' still I don't know why my grandfather named me so, maybe just because I kept on smiling when I was a baby, so-called happiness never travelled with me very long. I would say happiness plays a vital role in our lives. One cannot be happy all the time, there are some limitations for happiness; even my life had some limitations. When you say love, wow! What a powerful word, isn't it? It makes it more powerful when you say it from your heart and when you experience it. Love is another form of happiness without any limitations.

When I say without any limitations, it means no limit for happiness, which can change your life by any means. Everyone would have had the happiest moment in their life, I too had incidents which were really heartwarming. Love is God, a feeling which gives you happiness throughout your life journey from the time you were born till the time of your death. God cannot be seen, but he is inside you in the form of love. It took thirty two years of my life to understand the purpose of my life here. It may sound stupid, but as life goes on never forget that we are here to serve for a purpose. Every one of us been sent here or recruited for a purpose, until and unless you take an effort for yourself to know it. This entire book deals with the struggles I have been through my entire life, and why am I being directed onto a different path by someone I feel is unknown to me within. I may sound spiritual, but the fact is, it is more than that. I would also like to mention here that I never read any kind of novels or spiritual related articles, I have never been inspired by anyone. Can you imagine if I tell that I am spiritually involved now, who was once a non spiritual person? I was struggling so hard in life to figure this out all these thirty two years of real me. The incidents which I have shared in this book are not just imaginings,, they are my observations towards inner consciousness, an observation about what is happening in and out within you. The experiences which I had would have happened to you at some point of time, I am sharing it with you in the form of a book. All I need is to convey the message in a smooth way so that everyone can understand what I am trying to tell; whatever you feel is good for you, it can be followed or else it's up to you to decide, some may believe some may not. When I started working on this book I myself got into a dilemma, what am I doing here? Am I writing a book of my own, I have never dreamt of writing a book in my entire life. As I said, the very beginning is about the two factors, you can take it in either way, whichever is comfortable, but I would say it's me myself within, that finally came to a conclusion to write a book and finally understand the path given to me. I know I am confusing a lot, in the beginning you feel you are confused, but as you go on with this book your mind will be clear of questions. How can you judge a person just by looking at his physical appearance? You have to know him better, you have to understand him better, only then can you tell what kind of a person he is, just by looking at a girl or a boy then and there you judge his or her character, then it's wrong. I totally disagree, likewise the same applies to each and every book, just by looking at its cover or just by reading bits and parts from the book, will not give you a conclusion of the book, you need to dive in deep within the book, this is also like judging a person. In a book, a person brings his own emotions and character into it which will give you an idea about the author and the other characters in this book. Sometimes when I was alone, I used to imagine things which would never happen, even you will have done this, dreaming about things which you know for sure will not happen, but still you ought to do so, the reason is it gives you happiness, likewise in life too. Only if you enjoy doing things do you get happiness, I have spent my entire life without knowing what a person really needs in life in order to stay happy all the time, for some it may take only seconds, some may not be happy but they pretend to be happy, for some it takes a lifetime to know the fact and finally he disappears, happiness differs from person to person, though it took years for me to find the real truth of happiness, finally it led me to the divine happiness.

One day when I was sitting in my house I had an inner energy provoking me to write about something instead of spending time doing nothing, so I started writing about things which happened in my lif. All of a sudden I had a strange feeling within consistently provoking to go on with writing. At some point I forgot myself and became so much into it, like I already had a passion in writing, so I questioned myself why don't I make a book out of this? That's how I took this book seriously and started working to make it better. You know what? You will not believe it if I say I do not have writing skills, and I do not read many articles or novels for that matter. To be frank, there are no such hobbies in my life apart from doing nothing, most of the time I enjoy doing nothing, or the other way it gives me happiness. But when I started writing this book everything changed in life, that so-called change is what I am going to talk about, and also about love and an unknown master within my life. People say I have been inspired by these incidents, or that I have been inspired by someone special, it depends, but in my case I have never been inspired by anyone in my entire life other that the master within, and that too very recently. I know I am confusing, saying a master. You may think 'who is this so called master, what has he to do with this guy? I can guess what your mind is trying to ask, but before explaining about the master within I would like to tell you what made me realize there is a master within. Let's dive into flashback, you might have seen when there is a flashback in movies you will get a good background score, over here the background score is your heartbeat, and the place where you sit and read this, observe the music within you and with nature. You become the music.

When I started this book I was thirty two, only believed in himself, no spiritual interests, and a person who thought God did not exist. Everyone would have had the happiest and most memorable moment in their life, so have I, some are interesting some maybe not. When I say love you can remember so many things which come to your mind, without love we are nothing in this world. We are driven, motivated, responsible, committed and so on with love, beauty lies in the form of love. I too had struggles and problems in my life all these years. I am a lazy guy, you will not believe how lazy I am, but that's the fact, if someone asked me to do something for them I never took the initiative to help them or at least ask them what they really needed. When I was thirty one I got married, before marriage we were four in our family, I have a younger brother, father, mother and me that makes four. I had a job at the beginning, but now I don't have any job, recently I lost my job due to some personal issues. We say at some point in life we will get some kind of situations which lead us to peak, or which drown us totally, it depends on a person, what kind of situation he is in, but mine was second category – a time in my life where I was forced to by myself to issues at the same time happiness together. The time after, when I lost my job, it made me think of a lot of troubles which I went through in my life, I think everyone would have faced these kinds of situations in your life when suddenly the life cycle stops or starts applying breaks during the go, how that feeling would be, I too had the same effect in my life, but I started realizing what is right in our life when I started realizing the master within trying to teach me something which I was not aware of. Though I am from Kerala, myself and my family spent most of our life in Tamilnadu, starting from my schooldays till my professional life. As far as education is concerned in our family, in those days, my father did his Masters degree, which no one ever did in those days. My father is so interested in studies, it took an effort to do his, though his father was not wealthy, but if you take me I am just the opposite of it, I am least interested in studies. My father wanted his kids to do well in studies as all fathers do, but we can't expect things to happen in life whatever we wish to happen, so he had his own consequences. My mother is a typical housewife and my younger brother is a graduate, he stopped after that due to financial issues, though he had an interest in doing his Masters; unfortunately, life is not we expect, it takes some time to come to you, patience is required in order to be successful, which I believe in. I never had any interest in studies from the very beginning of my life. My mother never completed her tenth grade, she discontinued it, when we asked her why, she used to tell us in those days they never had any time to study rather than work for the family, the reason is in those days the family was very big, they had around nine to ten kids, imagine if a family had this many kids, they would never bother about children's education, as soon as they cross eighteen years of age they would get married. If it's a girl child in the family they never bother about her studies at all. Though my mother's family was wealthy, they were into farming and depended on agriculture, so all these kids had an equal responsibility in providing income for the family, so they never bothered about their education. Nowadays, the system is changed, everyone needs education, everyone is been treated equally, even the government of India insists on everyone's education. Altogether my family is sweet, simple and happy like all other families.

I still remember my mother telling me when my father married her he had no job; if I am not wrong he got his job after his thirties, till then my mother had struggled a lot, no one used to tell me stories those days when I was a kid. I have heard kids telling me that his or her parents or grandparents used to narrate stories to their kids during free time, I don't remember that happening to me when I was a kid, nor did I have a chance to hear those kind of stories, but I do remember my grandmother kept on narrating her stories in life to my mother when we were living together with our grandparents, that is the time I too listened to her stories with my mother. That's when I came to know about my grandfather. I would like to share some bits and pieces of his experience which I admired.

In those days, child marriage was at the peak, I still remember my grandfather telling me that he got married earlier before knowing what marriage was all about, I imagine marriage at early age is very difficult, but he had no choice those days, that was the system they followed, just imagine how the outcome of marriage would be, no time to understand each other, parents decided and they tied a knot and were declared husband and wife. Some marriages like that have been successful some not, but the government has taken so many actions against child marriage, but still in some villages they do follow these kinds of marriages, but mostly it's been stopped. The credit goes to the government of India. Though my grandfather got married early, they still had an awesome life, no words to describe it, they had a happy married life. Before marriage, my grandfather had some difficulties in life, he is a man of his own rules, he never used to worry about anything in life.

Everyone in this world is born without any dreams, but as they grow desires and passion grow, which includes good education, money, spending a luxurious life with the family, all these factors grow day by day as we grow, am I right? Even in schools they teach us that the three factors which a human needs are that of food, clothing and shelter, in order to get these we need money, which is the truth, but as far as I know my grandfather never had any desires or passion about anything, he had his own set of rules. All these years even I had no passion or desires, no one have ever noticed that maybe they never wanted to or they don't have time to, which never means I too followed my grandfather's footsteps, not at all, he was entirely different. But in some facts we do have some similarity. My grandfather was very frightened of his father, not only him, all his brothers too; he was very strict so no one liked it, but my grandfather, though he was frightened, he liked him a lot. Too much love at times will lead to a problem, the same happened to my grandfather; as days passed he thought he needed his own freedom to do things, so one fine day he wanted to leave his house and do his own work, so he left there without telling anyone. Most of the kids don't like fathers to be strict, some obey, some may not, and my grandfather liked his father but had no freedom so he left. Too much courage is not good if you don't know what world is outside, he had no idea what is he going to do after he left. He travelled a lot and finally reached Tamilnadu. In those days you didn't have to worry about any employment like we do today, so he joined a firm and started his life with full freedom, he had the job which he loved later, which made him get his life settled.

With his courage somehow he got a job which he thanked God for, whatever it is, when you leave from your house without telling anyone, everyday memories will haunt you. So after years he went back to his house and once again got united with his family, and got married and started his life in Tamilnadu. If you have the strength and willpower you can survive anywhere in this world without any help, this may not work for everyone but as per him it did work well for him, since he is a true believer in God he gave the credit to God. He was not literate, though he took an effort to learn things by reading a lot of books by himself. The place where he worked had British men where he would communicate only in English, which my grandfather was not capable of. Initially, he started his career as a laborer somewhere in nilgiris under a firm which manufactures tea, but sooner or later he became a supervisor with his hard work and excellence. Soon he started to earn well, learned to communicate in English with others. I have seen people who have been to convent still struggle to communicate in English, but my grandfather learned quickly, which is really surprising. He bought up his kids gave them a good education. He had five kids, two of them were boys, which includes my father as his second son, and the other three are girls, with a one man army not being dependant on others, he soon finished all their marriages too. But all these years he lived for his family and forgot to save for himself. He was a person who lived in the present, not past or future; he never worried about the future so he lived for his family till the end without any savings of his own. I have come across a lot of them in my life who spend most of their life in earning a lot of money and creating assets and fixed deposits, but this man was totally different from others, who never had any assets apart from his children, that was what he believed till the end. It's hard to find these kinds of people in this busy world, where people chase time and search for happiness, that's what we do now, we are running from problems each and every day rather than standing still and facing it. According to my grandfather, he knows only to love others and not to hurt, though he had problems in his life he never gave up, instead he fought life patiently, which I like in him, most of them do not like him because of the way he dresses; he was not modernized, he was typical. I always admired his honesty. I was not present at the time of his death due to some personal issues which I had, another bad episode in my life at that time, which you will come to know as we go on. My grandfather has never been an inspiration to me, I do miss him at times, I know for sure he love me so much, but in return when he really needed love I was not present. It was totally my mistake, I take the blame for it. He was into spirituality, I would say a strong believer in God and so dedicated. When he was alive I never knew his value, but after his death I recognized his true value. As I said, I was not at all inspired, but I always wanted to share that I loved him the way he was. When you become old some people don't like the way you behave but keep in mind even you will cross that stage in your life, most of us forget that at some point of time which we should be always aware of. You can learn what love is only from them because they know what life is.

No one is honest in this world, people do mistakes in life. I will never say I am perfect, even I have made mistakes, I have seen people not being responsible, but at some point they become responsible. If you take a look at my life, I have never been responsible when I was required to be, I have seen others telling me 'you are a complete loser in life and always incomplete.' All these years I have spent my life without any meaning. I am not an ambitious person, I don't have any kind of responsibility, not worried about anything, neither being jealous. I have seen that my colleagues and my cousins who grew up along with me are in good jobs and well settled except, reason is I am still playful and kiddish and not worried that I am not settled. I have seen people soon after their college getting into good jobs and good designation, who used to say 'this is all God's grace.' At that time I never believed in what they said, rather I said 'it's your luck.' To be frank, I never demanded anything from God like others kept doing. I faced my life as it happened happily without any complications, blaming myself for the consequences and not God. I have seen people blaming God for this kind of life, the reason is they are not willing to accept life in a smooth way.

People did advise me ,it's free anyone can do it. I know they are trying to be good, but I was least bothered about them, I did what I felt like doing, what my inner heart had to say, people have desires run behind popularity and fame, I never had any kind of desires, but at the same time I like staying, doing nothing, obviously parents will create problems if their son is not responsible. In order to avoid that I did work in companies. If I liked it I stayed, if not I would switch over. To be frank I have never stayed in one company for more than six months, just for the sake of my parents I worked, but my interest was not in professional employment, I never liked working under someone. I always wanted to do something of my own, at the same time not financially sound either. I never had many friends who could help me. Relatives often tell me if you work hard you can reach places faster than you expect in terms of money and good designation. I too agree, my point is you work hard your entire life and you earn a lot of money and get a good designation; finally you take nothing with you when you die. I had this question raised myself all these years – what kind of a person am I? Doing nothing when others are getting well settled, my parents, friends used to tell me set an example to others by looking at them, at least you try to change yourself, but I had no outburst to what they said, I still remain calm and patient doing nothing serious. You may think how come he is writing a book, is he creating his own stories? No, not at all, the incidents which happened in my life are the known fact. I would like to share something here which is very interesting. Imagine, suddenly God shows up in front of you and tells you I am the God that you have been searching for all these years, some people think whether to believe it or not, some think is it a dream, some still want to test his identity, we people pray to God for so many reasons and demand of him so many things, and he is right in front of you and you don't believe it, this shows how true you are to God, to yourself. The reason why I shared this information here is that I had an incident in my life recently where I felt my inner consciousness speaking to me. When I shared this to others they said it's superstition, some said 'he has no other work he is playing, how can it be true?' My question here is, you believe someone who agrees on the fact God does exist, why don't you agree to someone who says God does not exist? I am confusing, I know, but the fact is I am inspired by the Master who is leading me in a good direction. There is a human beyond human in everyone's life, that's the power you have in you, once you know the power to observe within you, you tend to act differently which is what I am experiencing currently. Still confusing, you may think what is he trying to convey here? It does not make any sense, you will get the answer as I share my experiences one by one.

People don't accept things quickly until and unless they do research on it, even I did the same, I never used to believe in things which are not believable until and unless I practically experienced it. I don't believe in God, but I like visiting temples and monuments, I like places which are calm and silent, it gives you positive energy when you are in some kind of stress; it relieves the stress and makes you free. So I often visit church, temples and even mosques. I don't sit in front of God the whole day demanding something or the other. I just feel relaxed when I am in places like that, I have almost been to so many places, visited so many temples all over India, I love travelling. I always wanted to stay happy, which I have followed sincerely all my life, without any complications. I too had some problems but I faced all of them without any regrets, which I would say is my plus. I never had many friends, I like spending time all alone, at some point of time I did work for some companies, but I never stayed there for long, the reason that never gave me happiness, I did my job honestly, only thing is I never stayed.

I have heard people telling me to work hard like them in order to grow on my profession, obviously if you work hard you get what you expect one day, not all of a sudden, you need to wait patiently in order to achieve it. The new generation don't have the patience to wait, they rush so fast and end up getting nothing, and they blame this on God. I have seen people accusing God for nothing at all, if something good happens then you praise God, at the same time if it goes wrong then start blaming, this is how humans behave. God knows what is right for you and what is wrong, he just directs you, but you need to have the patience to accept whatever happens in life, whether it's right or wrong. If you keep on making it big for nothing then you create stress for yourself, that's what I have seen most of them doing. So it's not only hard work involved, it is just secondary. First and foremost, you need to enjoy what you are doing, if not you need to have willpower to accept things else you end up disliking your job. I believe in satisfaction rather than hard work, if you love what you are doing without any expectation it automatically brings you happiness. All these years, I haven't got any satisfaction in the work which I do, nothing gave me the real happiness, everyone started to blame me, I was least bothered, but still I worked for my parents to make sure that I didn't hurt them. There were times I never had any job either, but still managed to overcome all of my issues very happily and smoothly. I myself had this question raised at times, 'why are you not interested?' In any other activities other than sitting all alone doing nothing when I am alone, what kind of a person am I? All these years I never make friends, I never had any interest in any particular thing, if at all I am interested I will not have an urge to use it until and unless I feel myself to be so. If you ask someone what are your interests, they will say I am interested in music, reading, cooking, entertainment and so on, each one's hobbies differ, in my case I don't stick to one thing because I don't know what my interests are. Whenever I attend a job interview when they put this question to me, I pretend to be interested in some facts, although I really don't mean it. To be precise, my life was meaningless until I figured out what life means to me. Now let's begin our journey

My schooldays were lovely; my father was so keen in giving his kids the best education he could like all other fathers in this world. When he was a little kid, he had no chance studying in English medium school, all the way he had to walk around five kilometers to school, he struggled a lot during his schooldays so he did not want his kids to follow the same, so he had a dream that his kids should not struggle in life and they should have a beautiful life. As he dreamed, he admitted his kids in English medium, though he was not that wealthy, he worked hard to give his kids the best possible education to help them. In those days, I seemed to be a brilliant student, that's what others used to tell me, but I never felt so, in school they followed a ranking system and I tried to hold up the first rank for almost five years till my fifth grade. As the years passed I started to drop down in studies slowly. I have seen fathers being very strict to their kids, I will not say it's bad, they are being strict for our own good, at that age kids don't have that maturity to think that their parents are trying to be good to them, not to blame kids for that, the reason is the parents don't know how to tackle their kids softly, so kids think that the parents are trying to pressure their kids to follow their rules. In this case we cant blame kids either, at this age they don't know what is good, as a parent we need to help them softly and give them the freedom to converse what they exactly need from parents, most of the parents never follow this, parents are matured, not the kids, so being a parent is not that easy. They need patience to follow their kids' footsteps, never demand from, instead learn and observe from them. My father was not that strict, he gave his kids the right freedom to do and learn things, that does not mean I can make mistakes, as kids we do make mistakes, but as parents when you see your kids making a mistake advise them what is right and what is wrong in a smooth way, that's what my father did, he gave advice instead getting angry with his kids unnecessarily. So I, as a kid of my age at that point, started observing my father being so nice, I was always happy in what I did, happiness has never disturbed me in anyway, which I also wanted the same. Though my father advised me, I took it in a way that he was telling me for my own sake, at the same time I was least bothered, but I was more frightened of my father than my mother, if at all I needed something I never used to converse with my father directly, instead would I tell my mother, it was quite easy for me. My father had faith in his kids that they would not do anything wrong or do anything without telling them. But life is not as we expect sometimes, good turns out to be bad and bad turns out to be good. It had happened to me a lot of time in my life. In a busy world like this, parents don't have much time to spend with their kids, they are always chasing life, it's not bad, all they are doing for their children, but what is the point when your kids are not happy with you saying that your parents don't have any time for you?. At some point, my father too was in the same state where he never had any time till his retirement, but somehow my mother managed it well, since she was a housewife she spent most of her time with us helping us and she has done it well till now. All I say here is that parents should always have an eye on their kids, no matter what age it is they should always be with them, in brief love them for what they are, never hate them, even the kids have the same responsibility. My father kept himself engaged three sixty five days for his kids to give them a happy life, so my mid school till fifth grade I was in one school and from sixth till twelfth grade I was in another school, both of them were English medium. Nowadays, in this modern world, everything is changed, it's a machine world, you have a lot of things – communication is better, mobiles, computers and there are lot of electronics which have made humans very lazy. It's an electronic world, electronics has made an easy life for the people, though it has its own advantage and disadvantage, people like to be in a modern world with all these things and live a luxurious life. At one touch life became so easy for new generations, if you look at them they will be without a book but not without a mobile, that's how life is leading us, they are always updated, always they try to update software on their mobile whenever new software arrives, likewise parents should always update their kids, feed them good things and make sure that they are on the right path, love them to the core. When I say give them the freedom with some limitations, freedom to do the right thing, which they feel is good for their life, before you advise them, make sure you the are perfect person to advise the kid, or tomorrow the same kid will question you for not being right. The world is like that, it's not olden days to keep on dumping them with olden ideas, they are learning to be new, parents are the ones to make sure they are doing the right thing and go accordingly. Now, you may think whether I have followed all this being a kid, no not at all, but I understood what parents love is all about. I am not the right person to advise, but I believe in the fact that a person who realizes and admits his own mistake makes him a real person. God lives with us in the form of parents; it depends on person to person to understand that fact which took years for me to realize the same.

I don't believe in God, you will see this phrase continuously in this book; the fact is that is the truth. Changes happen in life, when you don't realize those changes and act accordingly, you will regret later which is what my life taught me. You don't realize what are your strengths, you have something in you that you may not have realized, when you start realizing it you will know the truth of happiness. You can be happy till your parents have the strength and capability to help you out, just imagine after that if you still depend on your parents. Life will have no meaning till you find your own happiness and make others happy at the same time. I was happy all the time when I was dependant, then my life started searching for happiness and love, two simple questions, what makes you happy? And what is the meaning of love? Both are essential in life and then comes money, for me money has always been third, first and foremost is happiness and then love and finally money, without happiness you cannot love and if there is no love then there is no life and for life money is essential, Life is just a part of all three. Don't get complicated your questions will be answered as you flee with the experiences occurred in my life.

If you ask someone to talk about love they will have lot of things to talk about, love is something that each and everyone believes in, no doubt in it, at the same time if you ask someone to talk about God, a person who believes in God will have more to talk about. Both are same, but when it come to life they play different roles, I hope everyone is following me because once I too had the same confusion. We take love as one character and God has another, they are common in one thing, both cannot be seen, love is God nor God is love they don't have any other meaning, if a person believes in love he believes in God too. If someone asks you to speak about the topic love, everyone does have some or the other stories to remember, love not only means to your boyfriend and girlfriend, it can be anything, whatever you see in this world is love, whatever happens in your day to day life accept with love, acceptance makes love pure, you might have heard love is blind at times, you know why they say love is blind, it's not that you go blind when you fall in love, it is that you only feel it in the center of your heart. When you feel so, what happens is you feel so excited, happy , blissful and so on. At this time, you close your eyes and observe what is happening around, everything seems to be like music in your heart, even your heartbeat, I don't how many of you observed this feeling, but I have experienced this, it's a blissful experience and there are no words to explain unless you personally experience it. So as soon as you close your eyes and start realizing your outer world becomes blind and your inner world becomes bright and you will feel that you are in heaven. As you grow up there are different stages to be crossed like from school to college, then to career, and then your family and so on; likewise, even love has different stages, from parents you realize what love is, and then from friends and others so you start to realize love as soon as you are born, and it will start to grow on you as you grow. It will come to you disturbing you; you don't have to go searching for it. It happened to me, so I hope the same applies to everyone in this world. So love is in you and how do you realize it? He is always waiting at the doorstep and knocking, just let him in, he will do the rest; likewise God is in you, always calling since there is so much rubbish in your heart you cannot hear, just fill your heart with love and then listen, you will be able to listen to him. We search for God in temples and other sacred places, but he is in you searching for you to look at him, and we are not bothered to listen to his voice, he is always telling you to stop demanding and obtain silence, silence leads to him, not only God, even love. I had someone asking me recently to tell the difference between God and love. I asked in return 'do you believe in love?' he told me yes, and I asked him, 'on what basis do you believe in love?' he had no answer. I asked him 'why can't you answer?' He told me, 'whatever answer I give for love it's just not enough for love,' so I said, 'the difference is what we create, both

God and love is silent, you don't know when it will come to you, you are the question and you are the answer. You know when I was a kid, not only at that time, even now if at all I commit a mistake I ask myself so many times, whatever I have done is correct. I used to think in a different angle if I felt I did it wrong. I admit to myself, I take the blame on me, it's not necessary to share with someone, ask for help – you yourself are the solution, no one else can be a solution for your mistake. If you start to admit your own mistake, next time you will never commit that mistake again. Whatever you feel, it's good for your life. You follow it, never follow life with confusion, just follow what your inner energy asks you to follow. When you start to follow your inner voice for sure you are in your right way, in order to hear your inner voice you should be perfect to understand what is right in your life, only then will you be able to hear your inner voice. Once you start to hear it there is no way that you will be mislead, you need to take some effort to know it. In the very beginning, even I had the same problem to understand it, but later on I started to realize and still continued my journey. When you continue your journey to it, slowly you will notice a change in you where your ego will slowly disappear.

Occasionally my friends and relatives meet up, and when they look at me they used to say, 'you always seem to be in a confused state.' I always stay silent, whether outside or with my parents. I do not react to things faster; I have my own reaction to things when required. Society is what people are frightened of, you cannot stop them from predicting or assuming things, they always want to poke their noses in others' issues rather than theirs, if you keep on reacting to society's actions then you will have time to do that alone. Society is important, for functions or any other occasions not to interfere in your personal issues it's you have to decide of your own accord. Silence makes everything possible in life, when you start to react to a problem it will start to build up without any break. You cannot stop them from talking, but you can stop reacting to them. All you have to do is stay calm and go on with your life as it comes, one day you will be rewarded for what you are. You might have heard people saying 'think twice before you do something,' they are telling you to be aware because the world is like that. I don't believe in that fact, however you plan, whatever is going to happen will happen, no doubt in it at all, you cannot stop it from happening, but you can stop planning. Never hesitate to do good things in life by confusing yourself whether it's good or bad before doing it, whatever you feel is good for you, do it with your full freedom, even I regret a lot about it now. I used to plan a lot and never regret after doing it whether it has been successful or not, that's what life teaches us. Life says no past, no future, live in the present, never be judgmental, if you become judgmental then you will start judging for no reason and you end up doing nothing.

You may think this guy is going on advising, this is not advice, it's the known fact in my life, frankly speaking even I didn't know anything about this in the beginning, still I don't know anything, I just started to learn a few things. I have never been a good son to my parents, a husband, a friend, a brother, but I'm not sure whether I have done my entire role in my life perfectly, on my way to be perfect. There are people who act as if they know everything but don't know anything, at the same time people who act as though they know nothing, they know it well; you can see different types of people in day to day life if you travel a lot. You can see people reacting to problems which are worthless reacting to, people who advise us to be perfect who are not worth advising, rarely do you see people doing things full heartedly. According to my own experience, I wish to tell everyone things which you do should make you happy else never even try to do. You may start to think, now this guy is not at all talking about the subject, he is talking about something else, the reason is before starting to share my experience I just wanted to give a glance of the things which we know about.

Love, when we talk about this there is an extraordinary power in you; as I said in the beginning everyone will have some kind of experiences in their life; I too had some which we are about to look in, let's start the journey of love from a kid till I learn what true love is all about. I will not say my first love changed my life, but I would say it has been a stepping stone towards knowing love better. When you ask anyone for that matter, they say 'I cannot forget my first love, it was so nice,' you can go on praising it whether it is been a success or failure, there are incidents where first love changed their life , lost their life ,taught life and so on, you can go on discussing, love has its own meaning in different stages in life. When you are a kid you see love in your parents, you start to realize their love and you merge in their love, they are your first tutor of love. Then come friends, you start to realize in them and finally the people who you know from the beginning of your childhood till now are your loved ones. So love is started in you as soon as you are born, when the time comes to express the feeling you start to learn what love is and you keep on learning till the end, so define love, what is true love?

You know why they say we remember our first love? Because that is the first time you felt it from your heart – a sweet fragrance started to glow in your life, your thoughts become clear, imaginations and dreams happen for no reason, you go beyond the entire world and you stand alone with absolute silence, and you see yourself in it and get surprised and you ask yourself what made me change? The so-called change you see in you is what love is all about, this feeling will definitely strike each one of us in this world if the love is true. I call it a blissful state. It's not only love for that matter, it can be anything which you realize for the first time wherein your heart strikes your first bliss in your life you will never ever forget in life. No one can define love until and unless they have realized what love really means, because age is another factor in love. Love can happen at any age, but the question is do you have the maturity to handle love in a smooth way? True love is all about the truth in love, when I say truth there is no secret between two hearts, the heart is filled with love, it's overflowing with happiness, that's what true love is all about, in simple terms, how honest are you to the person you love?

I realized my first love when I was in second grade, now you may think why I called this love instead of calling it an attraction? You are right there is a reason, let's dive into it, you can love anyone or anything in this world at any age, that is your right, but make sure what definition you give for the feeling you call love, age plays tricks on you, but you need to ask yourself what is the change happening at that point, share it with your parents, if not you know nothing, that's what I believe in. There is nothing wrong in asking your parents, your first beloved friends who tell you what is good for you, and after that you can share it with your friends if required. Love teaches us to be dishonest at times, if you are not honest to yourself, only if you are honest to yourself can you be honest to the person you love, this is the main reason most of the love goes in vain people who pretend to be honest but they are not. Love teaches you a lot of things in life, when I say love here it's not only your partner, it applies to all you love in this world. I will not say I was like this, no not at all, but I learned things.

First love in second grade (I call it love) as you think attraction, it happened when I moved from Kerala to Tamilnadu for my higher studies when my father got a transfer in government sector in nilgiris" queen of hills". Yes obviously I was attracted to the girl; kids always get attracted to the beauty in whatever they see, they always love beauty, since I was a kid I got attracted to the beauty in her. She had an awesome smile and was so cute and fair. I was not the only one who got attracted to her, everyone in our class liked her the way she was. Whenever you talk about love there is another important factor you will not deny which is friends, they play a vital role in our life at different stages in life, some have best friends, some have good friends, and some have bad friends, according to me I don't categorize friends like best, good and bad, they are friends and I had least of them in my life at all stages in life. No one liked me at that time because I was not that active, I used to stay silent and calm all the time, I was very frightened at that time, a fear to express your own feeling. I am a person who believes that sharing your personal problems with others makes you more complicated in life when you yourself don't have the capability to solve it.

Though I was attracted to the girl in second grade I never had the courage to talk to her, even though she was in the same class that I was. I am not confident so you can imagine a guy like me will stay dump in class. I never used to participate in sports or any other activities in school, the reason was fear stopped me from doing things which I liked, but I never gave up admiring the girl, I kept on admiring her though I never spoke to her. Far from the place I kept on watching her beauty; though I did well in studies, teachers and friends hated me for what I was in class. Initially, when I joined mid school I was a little bit worried about communication and language, but later on I developed my skills. As days passed my liking towards this girl started increasing, but I never had any idea to convey this to her. This is childish love; at this age what else can you think about love other than beauty? Beauty makes love beautiful, her beauty made me realize the real beauty within and outside. She had friends, she talked to all of them in our class except me, maybe she would have thought it of no use talking to me, and even I was not bothered about it at that time, being a kid you will not be able to observe why others are avoiding me. I was not at all bothered about it, maybe I never felt it. I always wanted to be friends with her, chat with her, tell her about what I felt about her, but I never had any chance to convey this to her, the reason being I didn't have the courage to approach her and talk, that's how I was brought up. I take the blame on myself, the last bench student sitting alone in one corner, I still remember the class and the corner, it is still running in my mind when I am writing this. First love is not about the girl alone, it's about every single memory that happened in your life at the time of your first love, which is what makes first love precious.

Second grade love continued till fifth grade with not much difference at all, I just kept on admiring her, nothing changed except years passed, soon three years ran so fast I was still with the same fear of speaking to her, but I never gave up liking her. I had an urge to participate in sports at times, but never participated because of the fear, what causes fear? Nothing causes fear, you alone are the cause of fear. Most of them told me you are the same like your father, my father is less talkative, he talks only when it is necessary so they thought even I was like that, unfortunately that was the real fact. Three years still admiring the girl with no hesitation, can we call this love or like? Wait patiently to know what it is, let me come to the present situation

Recently I got married, it's been one year, it's not a love marriage it's an arranged marriage. Even after marriage I am still trying to figure out what true love is all about. Let's together figure this out as we go deep into it. Me and my wife are separated now due to some personal reasons, that too silly reason you will come to know as you move on. Define love after marriage? I happened to ask a colleague of mine to answer this question, he answered the question with a smile, first I was not able to understand what he was trying to tell me, then later on I understood that a smile means a lot either way, good and bad. I have seen so many of them in my life who can answer with the same smile if you ask the same question, the one and only reason is that there is no patience and no maturity. I realized this fact very slowly, by the time I started to see that my entire life was messed up. When I realized this was not going to help me out I never used to bother about it. After my marriage, my wife kept on insisting on one point that I never loved her. I don't know what made her to think so but she never stopped telling me that before and after marriage. I will never blame her, she has her own point of love, whatever she thinks love is, it is not what she get from me so the clash begins here. Then comes a villain character –I mean anger comes in, which makes the relationship more complicated and love fades away, this is what happens in every marriage. I will never blame anyone here because disputes happen, but I did not understand the real reason for a dispute. It's a silly thing that we got separated and I'm still waiting for the day she understands my love for her. As far as I have seen in all married life, disputes either come in the form of money, society, status, family members, and friends or finally love. When I say love here, yes, you are right, love can also be the cause for a dispute, it's not that difficult to understand what I am trying to say here. According to me love after marriage is what I call true love, in order to realize this fact it takes time, sometimes your lifetime or till the end you will never get the answer for true love. Me and my wife had so many issues from the very beginning, but I never gave up the love I had for her though I still couldn't stop her from leaving me. I don't know what my wife thinks about love, at times love gives you pain unexpectedly. I will not say my marriage life was not good, it was good, but somewhere I forgot to realize the truth of love. Honesty in love plays another role in life, she never lied. There were times people never trust me, I was not bothered or worried about it, at times I hid a lot of things for good which turned out to be bad most of the time. After my marriage I started to lose my hope in my life and started to search for happiness, though we are separated we are not divorced, I will not make that decision at all, although the mistake is from both sides I take the blame myself. We have heard marriage takes place in heaven, have you seen heaven? Heaven is what you see here, we make our place heaven, if love is there then that place becomes heaven.

I had a vision in my life that my marriage should be a love marriage, but life is not what we expect. I ended up with an arranged marriage. If you plan your life then life will start planning on you, for years I have been planning in life, for some it works, for the majority it will not work, like me. As years passed I understood what life had for me so I started to face it happily without any expectations. Marriage is a long process, either love or arranged, in an arranged marriage the total responsibility is of the parents, they decide what is good for their son or daughter, there is a system here that before marriage the groom will start a selection process in his horoscope, social status, girl and whatever is necessary, they start to match it with both of them. There is nothing to blame here because that is our tradition and culture, my question is, where is love in this? Love stays behind and comes in front only after marriage. Now in a love marriage, love plays heroism for the marriage, everything else stays behind. I have a friend who recently got married, it was an arranged marriage, this guy was in love too but I think that never worked out, so this guy's main hobby is every week he will go to a different bride's house and have a cup of coffee. Don't get confused, here in India before marriage there is a tradition where the groom will visit the bride's house, if the horoscope and the rest matches his preference, after visiting the bride's house the groom has to like her, and his family members have to. All this depends on the groom's and bride's family members, once everything is good they fix the marriage, this is the tradition, so this happened to my friend regularly for almost six months, either he was not happy or his parents, finally they happened to see a bride of their choice and they got married, and now they have disputes and are about to get divorced. So what is the point here going through all this when you can't stick to love? I don't know who found this system of drinking coffee in the bride's house. I don't get it, just with a coffee they make the decision. If it's successful well and good, if not imagine the bride's situation, nowadays even brides are not bothered. Mine was totally different. I don't believe in this kind of system, it was simple and sweet; you will come to know it later. Let's not debate which marriage is best, I just want to make sure where love is a subject for a love marriage, and love is an asset for an arranged marriage.

As soon as my father retired we moved from Tamilnadu to Kerala, since our native home is Kerala they thought they could spend rest of their life in Kerala, and so they started planning to get settled in Kerala by selling the house they had in Tamilnadu and with my father's retirement money all these factors gave them confidence to built a new house in Kerala. So they bought land and started to build a house. Unfortunately, there was no water on the land that we bought so they had to stop the work, everything was stopped one day, and that land became a burden to us when the plan collapsed. See what life had for us? Everyone started to blame us, obviously we could not stop them, all they knew was to blame. We never blamed anyone who helped us get that land since we had no idea about Kerala at that time, but still we thought it's not right to blame someone, so we were ready accept the loss and face life with full energy, keeping in mind that one day something would turn out to be good. I would appreciate my parents for this, losing a huge amount of money, though they were upset they never took it seriously, they faced life with happiness. They are happy in a rented house even now without any expectations, if it was some others in this state definitely something serious would have happened, we hear a lot of stories like that in our day to day life, but what is the point of being upset? Instead stay happy, which is what life tells us; you need to have a heart to accept things in life and keep moving in life without any expectation, life will automatically give you happiness, but for that happiness you need to wait patiently. The incident made us financially broke, you can imagine the outcome of the situation, obviously we were down, but never gave up.

My younger brother had a job at this time, being an elder brother I was doing nothing. I had jobs before this, but I never stayed in anywhere I was not interested, many started to talk about me being like this but I was least bothered about it. You cannot stop gossips, all you can do is not get deep into that gossip. I never felt happy working under someone, and I never knew what my interests were either, I started losing respect day by day, relatives and friends were talking about their children and were very proud of them. I was least bothered about all this, I know for sure I am not making my parents happy but what else can I do? I am not at all interested in working or interested in earning a lot like others. I myself don't know why? Most of my life I have never been complete in the journey of life, I cannot think like others and pressure myself in one profession and say this is my cup of tea. I feel complete only when I think this is exactly what I am looking in for all my life, till then like others say, I am incomplete in what I do right from my education till my life figures out what I actually require. One who worries about his own future will have so many complications in his life from the beginning. I am not worried about the past or future, just the present is what I think about, you may think my parents never had anything to say on this, yes they did most of the time all their life and they were fed up of doing the same thing again and again so they gave up advising. At times I have helped my parents, but ninety percent of the time I haven't made them happy, all I wanted was my own happiness, never to blame my parents, they still had faith in me, maybe that faith is still helping me to think about what my interests are. Responsibility is all my parents want from me. I am still fighting to understand what that responsibility actually means. Those who are reading this will definitely begin to hate me like others at some point, I know it, that's how I have always been. My parents had faith in me because they love me, let's see whether you too start to love me somewhere as we continue our journey here. Nothing showed up in my life, and my parents always seemed to be unhappy, so I started to work just to make them happy, even though I never liked what I did. I never had any passion for anything like clothes, jewels or any luxurious things in life like all the others did. I looked messed up, always friends used to ask me, "Why can't you even come dressed up properly and be a little modernized?" I never used to listen to them, I always wanted to be the way I wanted, friends started avoiding me for this particular reason, when I worked with other employers, I was not bothered at all. Do you remember me saying in the beginning what my name exactly means? I have always tried to be so in all my entire life, for others my life looked terrible and empty, but for me it was so sweet, I did enjoy the way I am.

Let me go back to mid school, three years admiring the girl I like never changed my mind, nor did I have the courage to talk to her, but I always wanted to show her how much I liked her. One fine day, I took a decision to share it with her, the reason being once I left this opportunity I would not be able to convey this to her in my lifetime, because the school where I was isn't a high school it is actually a girls' high school but till fifth grade they had coeducation. Keeping this in mind I started to build up my courage, by the end of this year I should somehow talk to her, patiently I waited for the day to come. At times school works on some Saturdays as well, where we are allowed to wear colored dress; a colorful Saturday came up in my life to express my love for her before I switched over to another school. Obviously, people who had their first love would remember the date and time, during their proposal they will make a note of it in their heart. Frankly, I have never made a note of it, have no idea about the date and time, but one thing which I noted was the weather and nature's expressions. I did make a note of that on that particular day, whenever you get excited or whenever you feel sad just go out and speak with, nature you will definitely see a change in nature.

Saturday morning, I got up early, dressed up well since it was color dress day. I never had a feeling of impressing her, at that age you don't even know what impression is. I kept my mind focused on telling her how much she meant to me. School is about two kilometers from my house, everyday I used to walk to school, I had a friend of mine who was nearby my house who joined me during the walk, he was a good friend to her who always sat with her in the class, he was looking smart in colored dress, whereas I am average, this is how you tend to think at that age, you get attracted in whatever you see. So I appreciated my friend for dressing so well and for being smart, just to make sure in return he did the same to me, so that I could be sure that I was smart; he never did that but I never bothered, focus was on that girl.

On our way to school suddenly the girl appeared, walking in front of us swinging her hands. My friend shouted her name, she and her friend who was walking with her suddenly stopped there after hearing my friend's voice. We approached her and she said hi to my friend and also appreciated him for the dress he was wearing, she never even bothered to tell me hi, I was walking behind when my friend was walking with her. Though we knew each other in the class we never talked much, my fear stopped me from talking to her. I don't know what stopped her from talking to me. Though I was behind them I made my mind up today, somehow, I would tell her about my love. Finally we reached school, the teachers gave us homework every day, and as usual my friend was sitting with her. At that age teachers never minded making girls and boys sit together on the same bench, my friend was always sitting with her, whereas I was sitting all alone in one corner, no one joined me even for a chat. That Saturday was very special to me because teacher made me sit with her on that day because my friend forgot to do his homework, so he was asked by the teacher to sit on the front bench. As soon as I sat next to her, I felt so happy, but she never minded me at all because she didn't like to at all; that never made me upset, I was happy because I had a chance to admire her so close, she was so beautiful with cute little eyes and smile, no words to express her beauty. She was always busy talking and she started to avoid me and often she asked me to go from there, the only reason I sat there was because teacher made me sit there. My friend was always coming to her place and did some pranks on her which she liked, whenever I saw my friend being so happy with her I too wanted the same, but I never had that chance at all. While sitting I tried a lot of things to speak with her, but she never wanted to talk, so I finally decide to move away from that place to go back to my place. Why get into trouble when she didn't want to speak with me? As soon as I left from there my friend came back to his place and she was happy; I liked it because she felt happy, she looked cute when she was happy so I always wanted her to be happy, as usual I admired her from far.

Saturdays were filled with fun sessions, teachers didn't take much class, we had lots of free time to draw, sleep, and play, and that too a half-day class. The teacher decided to take us out to play, so we went outside and the whole class sat under a tree, the weather was so beautiful and cold. Since its Ooty you can imagine how the climate would be, natural mists covered the whole ground, you would feel as if the droplets of clouds falling on your head would feel cold, but the mother nature's beauty is unexplainable, you felt as though your soul was travelling into the music of clouds; with all these feelings I started admiring her. You needed to see her face becoming pinkish as soon as mist fell on her. I was stunned for minutes looking at her face, can you imagine how nature brings out one's beauty? As I admired her, I suddenly heard teacher telling her "Your face became so pink," see what a coincidence? Even I thought the same, the teacher described her as looking so beautiful, which made her so proud. You needed to look at her smile which showed how happy she was when she heard that. I realized one sweet little thing, whenever you see a girl and appreciate her beauty she will be happy, but it should be true hearted and not just said for the sake of saying it. I really got carried away with the feeling, all of a sudden the teacher kept on calling my name, several times, I was not aware until the teacher threw a chalk piece at me and I suddenly came back to reality. Everyone for one second looked at me and laughed. I was not at all aware of what was happening there and suddenly the teacher was asking me to sing a song, so I thought it was some kind of fun session, everyone looked at me surprised to hear a song from me because all those years I had never even bothered to speak to them, so they were so excited to see me perform something. I stood still with no expressions for two minutes, the teacher repeatedly asked me to perform something, though I wanted to perform fear or shyness, whatever, stopped that so I never performed and the bell rang for the next period. So I was excused and we went back to the class. But I heard my friend did lot of cinematic dance and acted well in front of the class and made others happy, but I never knew anything because I was into another world. I was so upset because I never had a chance to speak to her at all. We had a few hours left for the Saturday class to complete and for a weekend to start before that I could tell her what I felt. As soon as we entered the class, the sky started weeping, I mean it started to drizzle outside. it was good to see the sky pouring gently, everyone in the class was so happy except me, my friend was talking to the teacher about something, so I thought this would be the right time to talk to her. So with full courage I stepped forward to her and called her name. She looked at me, that was the first time I looked at her face properly, and as she turned back her hair swung in front like a ponytail with two little tiny knots and her dress was sparkling. She asked me what is it? I don't know from I found the courage, I told her "I love you," without even knowing what that actually meant But still I expressed it and ran outside the class and my fear started growing like rain started pouring heavily. I looked at the sky for sometime and I was fearless for a while, The rain stopped slowly and the sky started growing bright which I liked, wherein I felt nature was trying to tell me something I couldn't figure it out. The wind was mild, which made me feel so happy, at that time I totally forgot the fear I had in me. I too was relaxed after telling her what I had wanted to tell her for a long time. I never bothered about what she would say to me in return, but I felt that something which was bothering me had found its freedom. Whenever you have something to express, never keep it with you, let it free, never bother about the result, let it free from you else you will always be in a confused state. Once you let it free then there you are free from so called tension, this is not only for love, as a matter of fact it can be applied for other things too. Never conclude yourself the story is over, it just began, just wait patiently to know what really happened after that, let's have a glance at my career life.

Before getting married, my career life was fluctuating. I did work in multi-national companies, but not long term career, it's just short term. I have heard so many of them telling me it was very difficult to get another job once you lose it, but for me it was just the opposite, very easily I switched over to another company as soon as I leave one company. The reason behind that is that I never took my life seriously, just blindly did things, it never ever affected me, but it did affect my parents. It's not because of the salary, it's not because I am lazy, it's because I never liked working under someone, I tried doing business as well, but that too never succeeded because my mind was never fixed on one thing. I never worried about money, all I worried about was my happiness, where would and how would I get a happy career, business, what else. I never got any answer, I continued my life in confusion, not knowing what would happen in the near future. Parents did ask me, "Why are you always jumping from one company to another, what will happen to your future?" They did advise me a lot, I was least bothered, if I took that seriously I would end up with another job where I would not stick again, so I stopped searching for job for a while thinking why should I trouble the employer? Relatives, friends and others started blaming my parents for my mistake, all these people didn't have the courage to sit with me and speak, instead they started bullying my parents. One thing which I hate very much in life is that if you have something on your mind just speak directly, never speak at the back of a person. Obviously my parents started to worry about me, the way I was, but I never worried about anything, there was no choice when my parents started compelling me a lot to get into a job.

One day, when I was sitting in my house, I happened to look at the newspaper that day, I was not into newspapers but still that day some strange feeling made me look into the newspaper and I found a job opening abroad for a customer service executive, which made me confident enough to apply for that job. I did send a mail and waited in return for an appointment for the interview. I never searched for any other job apart from that because I was not interested, and at the same time, I had the confidence that I would get the job which I applied for, something made me to think so. So I never googled for some other job, I have seen my colleagues searching jobs on the Internet and other media very seriously, so many of them asked me to keep on trying for a job, I never did that. Later that day, I received a call letter for the interview through email, which was send by a travel agency. This travel agency acted as a mediator for the client directly. My parents were happy seeing this because I finally did something useful and the interview was one week later, which was far away from my place. When I was attending this interview my age was twenty seven. All these years I worked but fluctuating, I would have switched over about ten to fifteen companies, if I am not wrong that's how I spent most of my career life, and this is the first time I was attending an interview for a job abroad. It's not because I don't like to work in India it's because if I went abroad I would stay for a long time in one company since it's contract basis so I thought it would be better for me to try that. I went to the place to attend the interview as mentioned in the call letter, and my father accompanied me since he did not want me to go alone. We reached the place the day before the interview. I was not at all prepared for the interview, even during my school or college days I never used to prepare, it's just the last minute study. I didn't plan, used to keep everything for tomorrow rather than doing it on the spot, that's how I always have been. The next day the interview was held in a hotel where the client did the interview directly, but before that the travel agency would select the candidates before appearing in front of the client. So I did well in the first round and was asked to go forward for the rest of the round with others. Around fifty to sixty were selected in the first round, there were thousands of candidates, and only sixty candidates were selected after the first round including me. Since the travel agency was totally involved in recruitment all they wanted was money from the client. They worked for commission because the recruitment is absolutely free, no cost involved to travel abroad, everything was taken care of by the client, that was what the advertisement in the newspaper stated. The client needed around one hundred candidates, already sixty were selected for the next set of round and all were written tests, the travel agents got a huge commission if one candidate was selected through them so just imagine if it was one hundred candidates. So they wanted almost all to get selected in the rest of the rounds because they needed commission and they were not that good a travel agency, they were just developing at that time. Before entering into the hall for the written test, the travel agency leaked the questions being asked by the client, and they shared the answers too, all they wanted was somehow for all the candidates to get through. Questions and answers were thoroughly discussed before entering into the hall, obviously it was easy, what shocked me was that though the answers were discussed, some candidates were eliminated. We had around five written tests, out of sixty candidates only thirty were selected for the final, which included me too. When all these rounds were completed there was no time for the final round so they informed everyone to come the next day for the final round. The final round was conducted by the client itself, face to face, so no question and answer discussing section it was time to prove your inner efficiency. Everyone was very clear that the final round would be the difficult one, and totally depended upon the client to select a candidate. We were asked to dress up in executive style to impress the client. I was not at all bothered nor listened to him, so we had to extend our stay for one more day. My father asked, "How well did you do for the interview?" I said with a smile, "It's OK," he was happy I guess .There were so many of them for the interview I never minded anyone nor made friends. The second day of the interview that morning, I was not at all interested in dressing up like an executive, but if I looked messed up my father would have a bad opinion, that he was not at all interested in attending the interview. So in front of him I dressed up well; I began marching towards the hotel, when I reached there I once again looked messed up. I don't get it, if I dressed well, would that mean I would get the job for sure? It all depends on individual performance, that was what I believed in whenever I attended an interview. Look neat and tidy, though you are messed. Thirty candidates were present that day for the interview, everyone looked very tensed except me, there was one guy who came near me and asked, "Are you not tensed?" I asked him, "For what? Why should I get tensed when I don't know what is going to happen, I am not here for the result, I am here for my parents." That's the answer I gave him and he never questioned me again nor liked me for what I said. As usual, I was sitting in one corner in the hall not disturbing others or communicating with them, when I spoke with them they would poke their nose in my personal info, which I didn't like to get involved in. The final round started at eight in the morning with four candidates, and six people were conducting it, two people, one candidate, the rest were waiting for their turn to come. The interview took forty to forty five minutes for each individual, everyone was frightened after knowing this. I sat in one corner waiting for my name to be called, when all the others were seriously discussing about what was being asked. One thing I was sure of is that you could cheat, and somehow I passed the rounds with the help of the agency, but the final round was all about communication. You would get selected only when you did well in communication, the rounds they had before were just testing your aptitude and your basic knowledge about corporate rules, but the real test happened in the final round. Even though I understood the fact I was not frightened, I still had the hope that somehow I would get through this interview, so I waited for my turn. I saw all the other candidates in there were referring to the candidates who had finished the interview, trying to grab some ideas to perform in front of them. When I was looking at them I was reminded about an incident which happened when I was in school, I was an average student, I never took studies seriously but I scored good marks. I had a cousin brother who was so serious in his studies he used to wake up early around three in the morning and he studied, somehow my parents happened to notice this fact, so my parents wanted me to do the same, get up early in the morning and study hard like my cousin brother. I hated memorizing text book, instead I liked reading once, but my cousin brother memorized his text book and read out loud so others could hear him. That's how he studied, he was so dedicated and serious. I tried it for sometime since my parents kept on shouting at me to be serious in my studies. I will not blame them because that time I was a little down in studies, that was the time I joined a new school where communication became so important. I was not that good in English at that time and that school insisted everyone communicated in English. Some days I would get up early pretending to study and I slept well, this happened continuously till I became steady in my studies. My parents thought I was studying so seriously with so much dedication, but the fact was that never happened at all. I soon woke up in the middle when someone approached me, asking me, where are you from? It was already eleven in the morning, I was still waiting for my turn. I could see some candidates praying to get through and the interesting fact about some candidates is that some of them already had a job but were still not satisfied with the salary they were getting, so they want to switch over. It's not because they liked the job they do or not, all they want is money. These people, they at least had a job, I didn't even have that so called job, but still they were worried whether they would get through this or not, but I had nothing to worry about. One thing I understood, people change jobs just for a change in their salary and not for their satisfaction. Salary was a concern to others, but I remember telling my parents each and every time whenever I change, the company's salary is not at all enough for me, though my salary is good it's not what I mean, it's because I don't like the job. I have helped my parents at times but that never continued for long as a commitment but as an interest, if I had to help my parents continuously I needed to stay in one company for a long while. I always remained bad for everyone, there is no change in that fact, even now it is still continuing but I am not bothered about that. When I came here to attend this interview, everyone else thought the same – that this guy is not going to be responsible or serious enough to get through this interview, but my parents still supported me without any doubt, that's the only reason I am here for the interview and it's already two in the afternoon. They called my name for the final round but unfortunately it was lunch time, so they told me to come after lunch and we had thirty minutes for lunch.

To be frank, I was not at all interested in this job, but I had no choice, I had to do something whether I liked it or not. I will be happy if I don't get through this interview, and my parents will be happy if I get through this. Lunch was already arranged by the company itself for the candidates who were present that day, so it was free of cost. I finished my lunch and was waiting outside the hall for the final round to happen. I looked at the others in terms of communication and experience, they were well versed whereas I was far behind them, but somewhere inside my heart I had the confidence that somehow I would get this job. I don't know what motivated me to think so, so I waited outside the hall with the other three candidates who were ready among six people, all four were Indians and two others were Americans. I was a little frightened because if these Americans called me I would be in deep trouble because I would not be able to follow their accent. Though I knew how to communicate, I still remember there were times that I had a hard time understanding the American accent, but now I can manage somehow. They called my name, I went inside the hall as I thought two Americans called me and asked me to have a seat, so I just sat and gave them the certificates which I had and the marks which I took in other rounds. By looking at that they appreciated me for the marks taken in other rounds, but I felt I was not worth kind of appreciation. I made up my mind to be honest with them and said that the marks which I had achieved were not my effort, they were the answers that had already been leaked before we entered the hall. In return, they said they knew it because almost all got good marks which was really weird, but they said they didn't care about the marks, all they cared about is the way you communicate, and they also informed me to keep it secret and they started explaining to me about the corporate rules and nature of the work. They asked me one question, "How soon can you join the company?" I said, "Whenever you want me to," and told them that I was not that experienced like others. I had never stayed in one company for long, only if I liked the job would I stay else I would move on, this is what I said to them. Within ten minutes my interview was over and they said that I was selected and they would let me know the joining date as soon as possible. I couldn't believe what was happening, within ten minutes the interview was over when for others it took forty to forty five minutes long for the interview, but I was sent out of the hall within ten minutes with a positive answer that I was selected. When I came out of the hall everyone thought that I was not selected because I just went in and came out so fast. I never spoke to anyone about anything, even I was not able to believe that I got selected just like that. As soon as I came outside of the hotel my father was waiting outside to know the result. I said I got selected, that I didn't know when they were going to send the visa and contract, but they said they would call me as soon as possible. I was not at all happy after knowing the result. I pretended to be happy in front of my parents, and I was in a dilemma thinking how I got through that interview. No one would believe this if I said this, so I kept quiet. If you know that you are selected after an interview, the first thing is you will get excited and you become happy, and you want to share this happiness with the rest of your friends and family members. I never did that but my parents did that on my behalf. Whatever, my parents were happy after hearing this. No one believed me when I said I got a job since I had a trust issue, some even said these kind of agencies are all fake, they just cheat people for money. Everyone started creating stories for no reason, they made my parents frightened, but my parents never showed it to me. The best part of the job was that we didn't have to pay any money for the job, the visa or travelling was all taken care of by the company itself. No one believed this either, I never had any proof that I got selected, it was said to me orally, not in writing or by an offer letter, so it was difficult for others to believe this at times, even my parents never believed, but I had the confidence, I waited patiently for the contract. Let's keep on waiting for the result here at the time same, let's have a look at the mid school love result.

Sometimes you feel love has no meaning. It's a blank feeling, never judge it if at all, you try to find out the meaning of love you can take a dictionary and find out the meaning of it for yourself, you will be clear, but when it comes to life you need a whole lifetime to figure it out, if you ask me what is love? I still don't know the right answer – as I said you can have a look at the dictionary and find the answer for it, but that's not it. Love is whatever comes to your mind whenever you see something, for example you see a flower that is one kind of love, you see a born baby that is another kind of love, so love depends on how you look at things. If you need a perfect answer you yourself have to experience it, love is God if you believe in God, love is in you and you finally express it to someone you like and you call it love, which everyone does. If that does not work as you think then you say that is not love, same person thinks in either ways, so it's not his or her mistake to blame it on love, it's the state of confusion one has. The excitement one has during love will not be stable as it goes, this is what we call a confused state, a state in which the mind wavers.

Mid school love is just an attraction. I fell in love with her beauty, when you say beauty or beautiful there is love in it, you say beauty only when you like or love something. So I said I loved her with full courage and ran outside the class because of fear, the fear was not because she would say no, the fear was because of the age. What if the girl goes and complains about this to the teacher? I had no choice, I had to enter the class for the last attendance, the teacher marked the attendance twice in a day, at the beginning, and the end. But the fear which I had in me was blocking me from entering the class, I just kept on thinking how I would enter the class and look at her. I did commit a mistake, every possible negative thought was running through my mind. When you start thinking deeper and deeper you tend to imagine things which are worse, but when it comes to reality it is nothing, still it is the mind that plays tricks on you. Fear is poisonous. I have had that poison in me all these years which is very dangerous, I was so quiet in class for three years, and all of a sudden if the girl goes and complains about me, what would the teacher think about me? Trying to act innocent in front of others, the next thing the news reaches to my parents' ears. All these thoughts were running over and over. I went to the restroom several times because of fear. Patience was all that I needed here, but I never had that patience to face her and the teacher. At this time I needed someone to help enter inside the class, the teacher was busy packing her bags, since it was the last period she was busy doing her work, so she never minded me standing out. All of a sudden there was another teacher who was coming looking at me, as soon as she approached she asked me, "Why are you standing out my dear?" in her sweet voice. I was so frightened to tell her, by looking at my face she thought I was about to cry, so she motivated me, gave me a hug and asked me, "What is your real problem my son?" Why are you standing alone here?" I had no choice other than telling her the truth, so I told her what really happened and why I was out. After hearing this she laughed at me and said, "That's no problem, go inside the class, I will speak to her." As soon as she said that I was very happy, and I was fearless. So she accompanied me to the class and she was discussing something with my class teacher and to the girls for a while, and everyone started laughing at me. I didn't know what they discussed, but I understood that they never took anything seriously and I saw a beautiful smile on her face which made me so happy. In three years she never looked at me properly, now she was giving me a cute smile and I was so happy to see that. If I had a camera at that time I would have taken a snapshot of her smile and would have kept it in my showcase. She looked so happy which made me happy too, maybe we were small children, no one took it seriously, everything, even my proposal was a funny incident. This is how love can be treated at that age, but whatever it is I still admired her a lot, nothing changed me from doing that. A kid who did nothing in that school and was not active and bright, suddenly made everyone laugh with one incident which made me think even I could give happiness to others rather than sitting silent doing nothing. At least I made everyone laugh.

It was time for a sweet weekend so everyone said bye to each other and left, and at last the girl for the first time said , "Thanks." I didn't get why she thanked me and also said, "Bye, have a nice weekend." I was like flying in the air, and was so happy to hear that from her in her sweet voice. At the same time the teacher who solved this came to me and asked me to do some small homework, that is to write a small essay in English regarding the incident which happened today, but in return I said I was not that smart to write an essay in English because I didn't know how to form sentences, but she insisted me to do this, so finally I said I would do this if I had time and then she left me with a small hug. In those days everyone liked me for my innocence, teachers used to hug me and show their love, my first encounter in my life was to write an essay in English, but at that time I never took it seriously. I liked that teacher for one reason – because she made the girl think about me, even though she never took any class or subject for us, she used to substitute for other teachers. In an unforgettable moment she finally spoke with me so from next the time onwards I could speak with her and be her friend.

For today's generation, if I had to explain the above incident they would call this love, after proposing to a girl and if she thanks in return then there comes love from that stage itself because that's how the world is moving, it is moving so fast, generations are so more advanced that love is like applying for a job, if you get it you stay, else you quit and search for another. We are in an electronics world, love becomes so easy it becomes a question and answer section, do you love me yes or not? I will not blame the generations, love became modern but the meaning remains the same, maybe the younger generations can change its meaning but love cannot be changed which is what I understood, but for me I couldn't think anything more apart from friendship at that age. I was happy that I could speak with her. As I said love remains meaningless until and unless you try to make it meaningful. So my weekend blossomed with sweet little memories and the fragrance of flowers, which made me think again and again of her, and I was eagerly waiting to see her back on Monday. Whenever you wait for something you will feel as if the time is running very slowly, am I right? Yes, I too felt the same, my excitement was overflowing, my mind kept on thinking of her, to speak with her, to be friends with her. Sunday seemed to be long for me, I even thought if they had classes on Sunday it would be better. This is how you tend to think when you are happy, happiness is good, if you are happy everything seems to be perfect in you, you will not have any negative ideas, that's how happiness treat you, it is a good medicine for all your sufferings. At the same I had a task of writing a short essay I was thinking whether to write it or not because my language was terrible and at the same time I even thought, 'Why don't I give it a try? Let our thoughts be free from imaginations for sometime and let's begin with my high school journey.

High school, a place where emotions meet up, a proper channel to learn and observe, bricks to challenge and face life in a better way, altogether you cannot point to even a single day without happiness, a place full of fun and joy, where life's happiness is met and there is zero tolerance to sadness. High school life is something which no one will ever forget, sweet memories, maturity, a total life blasting years for those who really enjoy school life and being with friends. I can tell that my life entirely changed when I entered high school, learned good and bad equally, new friends and teachers, totally a new experience. Before entering high school I was not that comfortable, but as days went on I started to like it. If I start to like something I go unlimited, will not stop until and unless I want to stop, at times I have got into trouble because of this. I was so silent and quiet in mid school, but when I was in high school it was just the opposite. I made my parents go mad on me most of the time. I noticed a change in me, a drastic change as days moved on, silence became my enemy and I started to become naughty and mischievous; we change according to the situations and environment that we are in. My parents couldn't believe the change I had, they have always seen me inactive and not charged, and all of a sudden they see me active and charged. This is what we say, character inside a character, we don't know how a person acts at times so it's hard to judge a person by his physical appearance, he will not be the person you think. Likewise, I too, started to change.

The high school which I was in was located in a district called Nilgiris which is in Tamilnadu. I believe most of you all would have visited Ooty, which is known as the 'queen of hills'. It's one of the best tourist spots to be in, and the climatic conditions are really awesome. My school was located on the top of the mountain and had a good scenic view, and the organization was owned by a British corporation internationally, and all the teachers and professors were non Indians and mostly were Australians, and very rarely did you find Indian teachers and professors. My father chose this school for me, maybe he chose that school because it was nearby his office or maybe he would have chose it after consulting with others, or he could have just like that fixed that school since it is an English medium school, whatever, school was pretty good with highly qualified teachers and professors, and English is an compulsive language. My father was very adamant to give his kids the best education and that too in the English medium, so he would have believed that this school would make his kids improve in communication and language fluency. It's not only the teachers who were from other countries, but also the children were from different countries, ninety five percent of them were from other countries like Tibet, China, Australia, United states, Malaysia, Singapore, Ceylon and so on, and very few were Indians, the syllabus they had was very difficult, but it was quite interesting to be in this kind of school where you have a chance to meet different kinds of students under one roof. My entire life from sixth grade till twelfth grade ii was in that school. It was an Anglo Indian and a mixed culture school, which was not that comfortable and easy for me at the beginning, but what made me change? That's what I am going to share in this particular segment, but before that:

What is school? Even in this definitions can be categorized by age, at different ages people have different opinions about the school they studied in. It can be defined as a place to play, a place to make new friends, a place to be innovative and to become knowledgeable, a place where your childhood memories are kept, you can go on explaining about school but for me I would say a place which made me think about the meaning of life and love. At that age I was not able to realize what was happening around me, but at this very moment when I started to write this book, I realized those days were very special to my heart, which made me realize the true meaning of life through the journey of love. Now you may wonder what love has to do with high school.

Mid school love, the whole Sunday went off quickly, thinking what to write and finally I did nothing. I am not kidding, the truth was I never had any idea to write because I was not that good in English and never tried to write because I was too lazy to give it a try. I felt very easy when explaining the incident to the teacher because I did it in Tamil, the language was easy for me to explain at that point of time, but in English it was very difficult. Monday, the next day, I was so happy to go to school, keeping in mind that it was a new day for me to be friends with her. After a long three years I had a chance to speak with her, with that in mind as usual, I walked with my friend to school and on our way she too joined us, she was happy and her smile was very cute as always, but I felt the fear in me whether she would talk to me or not. But things changed, she started to talk to me, usually what happened was I used to walk all alone, she used to walk with me holding his hand, but it was just the opposite, she was walking with me holding my hand and she kept on talking with me, and she became so friendly just because of that incident. I don't know what made her change like this. Situations make a person react, which makes a person either a hero or villain, my friend started to dislike me for becoming friendly with her, wherein I started to observe some kind of strange attitude from my friend. I didn't want to hurt him either, I knew that he never liked me talking to her, at the same time he was the only one who used to talk to me when others were not talking to me. I knew him well, so I knew both of them equally so I didn't want to hurt either of them. As the days passed she became so close to me in school, and on the other hand my friend started to avoid me for no reason, so one day I asked the girl that "My friend is avoiding me for being friend with you, what should I do to make him happy?" She said, "Don't bother him," but I couldn't do that. Though we were close I never used to sit with her during class, I used to sit on the same last bench all alone as always, though she asked me to sit with her a lot of the time I never obeyed her because I wanted my friend to sit with her as usual. My friend was totally changed after me being friends with her. It was hard for me to understand why he was behaving like this, but soon or after he himself came and spoke to me very happily, that was the day when the half yearly results were announced. He was the topper in the class and I was third and the girl was second, he was so happy that he became the topper and the girl was second, in class teachers appreciated them for being the best students in the class sitting together and studying well. My friend liked that appreciation, so he came and spoke to me. Both were very happy, I too felt happy looking at them smiling, but she never appreciated me, instead she became so close to my friend after that, she always liked to be with students who studied well, so they were topper in the class, and slowly she started to avoid me, and my friend liked it, which was exactly what he wanted. Now both were happy which is exactly what I wanted but something was missing all the time, which was my happiness. When you want others to be happy you should know what they really need from you to make them happy all the time, so I thought giving up my first rank for my friend would make him happy, at the same time I never thought she would avoid me just for this. As days passed the teacher who asked me to write a short essay on that incident forgot to ask me, maybe she would have forgot that so I never bothered about it at all, for boys and girls only till fifth grade is what they had in that school, so this year was the final year for my mid school life. Keeping that in mind, I tried one more proposal to her, and tried to speak with her in a friendly way, as she did for some months. I wanted to have her back with a cute smile, at the same time I did not want to hurt my friend, so the story returned to the beginning once again.

As usual I started to admire her from afar like I always did, at the same time I managed well to keep up my friendship, but she started to insult me for no reason for dropping down in my studies, even my teachers never liked me, it's like you made a big mistake. Teachers thought that

I started to drop down in studies, which is the truth, instead of concentrating on my studies I concentrated on others' happiness, which made me realize what real happiness is. The attraction remained the same but consequences differed, all of my teachers had faith in me, that this student would perform well in studies; when they saw my friend performing he became the best student along with her. I never thought all this would happen just because I gave up my rank, all I was thinking about was that I wanted both of them in my life without any complications and trouble. But it was not what happened, instead it developed more complications in my life, but I never gave up. I was least bothered about it with the same energy I started from the first. My friend was very good looking and handsome, he was not like me, he was so fat that no one could hit him, and everyone was frightened of him, the way he was, and he always made everyone happy by doing some funny things. That was the only reason everyone liked him, but he was not into studies, he was always behind me in ranking, but everyone likes him for his smart work. When he became the topper, he became more and more careful to hold that position for a long time. He started to do well in his tests and other activities in class, whereas I was dropping far behind. I didn't know what made me to drop down, though I studied well teachers began to shout at me, students began to laugh at me, initially when I was alone I never felt this loneliness. I did well in studies which made me different from the others but now I started to feel loneliness. I felt that everyone started avoiding me, though they did from the very beginning I never felt bothered, but now I felt it. My friend started to avoid me when he was in peak performance. I did this for my friend to make him happy, just not to avoid me, but when he became happy he started to forget me and the girl became very close to him. I was frightened of my friend at times, if he got angry you couldn't speak to him, he would hit you and those days I was so lean that if he just bled I would fly. I was like that, I knew how he reacted when he was angry, although I liked him he was the only one who spoke to me when others didn't like to, and he had a girlfriend who was his uncle's daughter, she was very pretty and he told me several times that he was going to marry her.

Whatever happened, I never gave up admiring her, what do you call this feeling of love or attraction, just keep on guessing like I did all the time? Final examinations were approaching, teachers kept on insisting that I did well in the finals. At least I never bothered apart from this, what I had in my mind was that somehow I should speak with her once again with full courage. Her plans were to continue in the same school since it was a girl's higher secondary school after fifth grade, whereas in my case I had to switch over to another school. I made up my mind once again to tell her how much I loved her during the last day of our final examinations, so I waited for the day to approach. I did all my exams thinking of the last day of the exam to come so that I could speak with her once again, but she totally avoided me. Everyone was busy studying for the exam, so no one had much time discuss with each other, even my friend never discussed with me or took a chance to speak with me. Finally the day arrived. I usually had a chance see her in the morning or after the exams were over, because during exams our class students would be shuffled to different classes I never had the chance to sit with her in the class where she was sitting during the exam, but instead my friend was with her in the same class, they were together each and every time. Luck will not knock your door when you expect something, luck is something which happens unexpectedly, you actually don't know when your life will have a so called turning point.

The last day of our final exam, I was waiting long enough for this day to come after our friendship got messed up for silly reasons, this was my final chance to tell her how much I was going to miss her and how much I adored her. So as usual I took a walk to school, since it was the last day my friend joined me for the walk after a long time, which I felt somewhat disturbing because I would not get the chance to speak with her if he came with me. I had no choice to tell him to go away so I made up my mind to wait patiently to know what really happened, this was my one and only opportunity to speak with her, even if I didn't get to speak with her I could at least see her smile, it had been so long that I had seen her smile. With that anxiety, happiness and paticnce to see her all of a sudden my friend called my name and said, "I have something to tell you," so I asked him what it was in a very low voice. In return, with a very rough tone he said, "I know you are behind that girl for a long time, I have been watching you for some days, but she doesn't like you because you are not smart like me." I stayed quiet, listening to him with no reaction and he continued saying that the girl liked him a lot, and he knew her mother very well who taught in the same school, so never try to disturb her. "If at all I come to know that you are disturbing her I will not be your friend," and finally he concluded, saying "she is my girl, and don't tell her that I said this to you." I was totally shocked hearing this, what did he mean by 'she is my girl?' What made him think so? Though he had a girlfriend, I had zero reaction when he said this because I knew that was not the age to fight for a girl, but instead I was frightened of him, his father was a dada in that area, if at all he told his father then that's it I would get into trouble, so I was frightened of him. So he asked me to stay away from her and to stay away from him. I had never seen him as my enemy in all those years. I had seen him as my friend and I had helped him a lot, now he was seeing me as his enemy. So I told him, "I will not come in your way. I will walk behind you all alone." Hearing this he was happy, and even I felt happy too when I saw her coming from afar. Seeing this, all of a sudden, I got a pinch in my arm and I woke up and saw my mother was in front of me telling me to get up from bed that it was already time to go to school. This was a dream visualization, so I was happy once again thinking nothing was real. My mind was once again reminding me that the final day of our exam was here, and at the same time the final chance to express my love, with the same energy I was getting ready for the exams. When I sat for the breakfast I started to remember the dream once again so I got frightened once again. I asked my mother whether dreams are true, my mother answered with a smile, "Some dreams are true, some maybe not, but most people say whatever dream you see during the morning hours, sometimes become true." All of a sudden my mind stopped working, the dream which I saw was in the morning, my mother asked, "Why are you asking me this?" In return I said, "I saw a dream in the morning, I just want to know whether it will be the same as when it happens." She said, "It may or may not happen," and then she never asked me anything, nor did I stay to explain the dream in detail.

It was already time for the exams, usually every morning before going for the exam my mother used to tell me to pray well and leave for the exam, basically I never used to bother about it, but today I thought it would be better if I prayed, though I never believed in God. I started praying to God, "Oh God, please help me to make this dream come true." And soon after I stepped out from my house saying bye to my mother I noticed that my prayer was wrong, if you look at that phrase you will understand, but I never bothered, thinking God didn't have any other work to do or not apart from answering my prayer, so I never believed in that it was my mistake in praying, since I was not used to praying. If you pray keeping other thoughts running over, then you will end up blabbering something, that's what happened to me. I prayed just for the sake of praying. Though I never believed in God I used to drop five rupees in the charity box which is kept in the church on our way to school whenever I had money, or I used to give those five rupees to a beggar who was staying nearby our school gate. So I took a walk towards school, I passed my friend's house, no one was there, the door was locked and my friend was not there, according to my dream he had to join me during my walk, so thinking that the dream was not true I just walked slowly, and all of a sudden my friend called, standing in front of a shop and said he was waiting for me. Now my heart started to skip a beat, by seeing him I fell in the open gutter, I broke my legs but I never felt the pain, instead I was thinking about the dream. I could see my right leg had blood stains and my dress had become dirty, but there was no reaction, I was in another world thinking about something else. After sometime I realized that I fell down, and there were people who gave me first aid and cleaned me, and that was not that serious, but I started to feel the pain in my right leg. I began to walk very slowly, my friend was walking in front without helping me at this point, but I never gave up and walked fast as I could to see her smile and to speak with her. With that anxiety I started to walk, as I walked I became confused whether my dream would become reality, I know you are very eager to know the same, let's walk together to know that. Patience is the key to success.

I would like to share about someone who I adore so much in my life, more than anything in this world, it's none other than my wife, after marriage and before marriage we had so many complications, not in love but in life. It took months for me to overcome it but life had something else for me, we were still sailing in the same boat of complications. I am reminded about a story here, there were two couples who were sailing in two different boats, both of the couples were newly married, and they were enjoying their honeymoon period. Both of the couples were happy sailing, suddenly the weather started to change and there was heavy thunder and lightning and the sky started to pour heavy rain and their boat were about to sink; though they had emergency services in their boat, at that point all they thought was to somehow escape and look in for a place to be safe, but they couldn't find any place and the boat was slowly filling with water and the rain became heavy, surprisingly both the couples didn't know how to swim; one of the couples decided if at all we die we die together, and they held their hands very tightly, the other couples were in a state of confusion who was going to die and they started to fight, see both the couples were newly wed, but in which couple did you realize love? Unexpectedly, neither of their boats sank in water, but the couple who fought created complications in life, love after marriage is a bit complicated if you don't know how to get committed or sail in the boat of love together, else it will slowly drown, but keep in mind you can still survive. It still depends who will survive, one who knows how to fight the situation will survive, and if there is love, one will fight for both, if you know the path to survive, my love boat is drowning still finding myself a way out because the other one already left. There is no such thing called complications in life, we create such things, but if there is no complication life is just an empty vessel, never complicate things, instead overcome them, I know it is difficult. I myself personally experienced it, but you have no other choice other than facing it. I faced complications rather than leaving it to others, when people get into trouble they tend to get into more trouble, the reason is fear to face it. I too had the same situation, but life had another twist. Once there was a disciple who asked Jesus, "What is the difference between your world and the world we live in?" Jesus answered the disciple, "Nothing much, you follow time, in my world there is no time." Likewise, if I had a time machine I would go back and fix all the problems and mistakes that occurred in life and start again, which is not possible, that's why we regret after we commit a mistake, the reason is we do not fix it then and there and we leave it to time to decide it. We tend to think like this because we follow time. As Osho said, "Never worry about past or future, just live in the present," but we don't tend to live in the present we always live in either the past or future, that's how the world is, likewise, I too lived in the past and for the future like all others. Me and my wife both equally created complications, now let's see how these complications started, before that you need to know my wife better.

Long black hair, slim, egg shaped eyes, fair complex age twenty four from Kerala, altogether beautiful, that's my wife – she is sensitive, angry, humorous, lazy, responsible, you can keep on describing her, but one think I will stick on is that she is very lazy I have never met a character in my life other than her in my entire life who is so lazy, I do not mean that I don't love her, I still love her for what she is but that's how she is. Some characters cannot be changed, it will grow on as you grow, you cannot change even though you try hard to change. If she is angry then she is beyond what one can expect, she becomes the ruler to the entire world, that is how she tends to think; at the same time, if she is in love then you will be surprised that there is no other girl who can beat her love, each day she comes up with new character, wherein it will make us go crazy thinking what she is, she is a confused puzzle, that puzzle made me puzzled too. I know now you are puzzled, the reason life is always puzzled is you don't know what comes in first, when you look at the mirror you see yourself and the first thing you see is your own eyes, and then comes the rest. Without eyes you can't even see yourself in the mirror, so eyes are important to see. Likewise, love is very important in life, when you look at yourself in life, love is what you see, instead if you see troubles and problems then there is no love. Why do people look at the mirror? Just to make sure they are well groomed and tidy, the same applies to life as well, look to it everyday and figure it out how tidy your life is. Why do you need a mirror if you know for sure that you are tidy? Likewise, you know for sure life is going to be with some turns and twists, just face it as it comes, you don't really need someone to help you out like a mirror helps you in knowing your own beauty. Your beauty lies in yourself by birth itself, you don't have to check it or modify it, this is how you are. The reason why I mentioned this here is love becomes real when you accept the beauty, each and everyone in this world has their individual beauty, which we don't accept sometimes. What I am trying to say here is accept life and love as it goes.

I never fell in love with my wife just by her beauty, there were reasons behind that, to make it clear you need to know her, we had nothing in common, whereas individual interests, likings, hobbies, vision, mission concerned entirely everything differed from each other. I have seen people leaving a relationship if they feel individual liking does not match, as far as I am concerned love starts only when you have nothing in common. That's what I believe in love, when it comes to sexual relationship people don't have any mismatching, when it comes to life people look in for matching. Matching is what we make in order to make life easy and free, boys always want girls to be under their surveillance, even girls can do that there is no problem in it, both have equal rights, it's how you go with it. Matching, physical appearance never comes in love it is not the quality of love, love has its own qualities.

Before marriage, even my wife had a divine love story of her own, though she looks modernized within she is typical, she is average in her studies because she hates working under someone, no particular vision or mission in life, middle class family, rather I call it a good family. I don't get it in here why we are categorized like an upper, middle, lower class family from the very beginning, this has been followed, nothing can be changed, but the thoughts can be changed not the rule so automatically rule becomes void. I am a person who follows no rule, who thinks not to categorize, but I too have experienced differentiation in public as well as private sectors. As a matter of fact in my family too, but that's how the world is seeing us. We cannot change the world, but we can change ourselves. For people life has become a choosing business, people choose the best in their life, it has become that we cannot act in life without choosing whether it is career, love, marriage, studies whatever they need the best of it whether they like it or not. Best here is categorized in terms of money, whatever helps people to improve his or her income turns out to be the best, so the formula is being followed when choosing their life partner. My wife did the same, but instead life gave her something else which she never expected.

As I said she has a sweet and very strong love story, she is the youngest in the family, she has an elder sister who is now well settled abroad with her husband, before her sister's marriage she was in love, love is dangerous, I have heard most of the boys saying this because they make it dangerous, else it's a beautiful feeling. Boys always want to rule girls, at the same time if girls start to rule then it will become dangerous and they have a lame excuse that it's not our tradition for a girl to rule, not at all keeping in mind that both are equal partners and they have equal rights. If there is love, there are complications, she too had complications because when you fall in love you just fall, you are not ready to accept complications. She was not ready to accept it but she fell in love. She is the one who taught me the difference between love and life. She used to tell me that love is meaningless all the time, why people ought to say this, because they can't justify love if it goes wrong, at the same time if it succeeds then love is meaningful. We hear people saying behind every successful man there is a woman, maybe that's true, in my case I too wanted the same to happen.

She follows her own set of rules in her life, she doesn't like anyone interrupting her path, she keeps herself engaged all the time with some or the other work, as far as I observed all these qualities were seen in her before marriage, and she always used to mention that her vision was not to work after marriage, she always wanted to be a perfect housewife. Her life was fun filled and sweet before marriage. I said that she too had a sweet love story to remember before getting married, the love story started when she was in college.

Before getting into so called love she was a person who hated love, she had seen her friends getting into trouble falling in love and fighting for love without parents noticing it, which she dislikes. She loves her parents and she is so close to her parents, whatever happens in her life she used to share it with her parents, they were so close; she follows honestly what her dad taught her from her childhood, she is so close to her father rather than her mother, and her family is not financially sound so she knows what difficult is, so she made up her mind not to hurt her parents in any way. Her school life was not that impressive, because as I said, she was not at all interested in studies, just because her parents compelled she was into it. Her college life made her think a lot about her life till then, even though boys proposed she never used to bother. We think girls' lives are easy, not at all – as soon as they grow up they have to face so many difficulties in life, they have to take the utmost care in each everything they do nowadays, even in schools they have to be very careful. If a girl doesn't have the courage to face life then it will be a serious issue, if she has the courage she can overcome any difficulty in life, at a certain age girls need to wake up and be strong to handle things in a smooth way. Girls have issues right from school till they get married, for that matter even after marriage it depends how girls react to these kinds of problems. I have heard boys telling me often that you can't believe girls, it's not the belief it's because we don't try to understand them.

When I say this, I would like to share a small story that happened to one of my friends, my friend was in love with a girl when he was in college, their love continued for seven years right from college, they were very true to each other, they had a true mission to make their love successful so they shared their story to both of their parents and everything was going fine. Both of their parents accepted their love by seeing their sincerity in love as well as their life. Both of them had a very good career, everything in their life was running smoothly. One day the girl's parents met with an accident and they died on the spot, on hearing this girl was shocked and she was not able to concentrate on her work or do anything, till then the boy's parents were very supportive, they helped her in many ways, since she was the only girl in her family her relatives thought somehow if she finished her marriage she would have someone to be with her, instead staying alone, all the girl had was her single small house alone, nothing else apart from that, so her relatives knew about her love for the boy and they went to the boy's house and said their opinion. In return the boy's parents said that they needed some more time for the marriage, not so fast, but the girl's relatives tried to convince the boy's parents as much they could. But they never agreed, instead they said no. In the meantime this girl was very upset after this shocking incident, she had lots of responsibility and commitment in her so she never had time to speak with the boy she loved. Her situation never gave her time to be with the boy she loved, but the boy never tried to understand her, all he wanted was to spent time with her whenever he required it, which was not possible for her. This continued for a long time, which made the boy doubt her. Instead of helping the boy started to create complications, since the boy's parents never agreed for the marriage, all of a sudden her relatives tried to convince her for another marriage soon because she was all alone, and the boy who loved her never even helped after her parents accident. In a girl's point of view the girl started thinking about her life whereas the boy never thought about her life, instead he started to think about his life, which one do you think love is? I would say helping the girl when she actually needed someone at that critical situation is love, instead blaming her for not calling, giving lame excuses is not love, that's what the boy followed, even his parents never tried to understand from the girl's point, all they wanted was for their life to be happy. So finally that girl married another guy due to her relatives' compulsion because she had no other choice, but the boy started to create problems saying that the girl cheated for some days. He kept on saying this to everyone, and then he stopped at some point and he went abroad and got well settled with his life and then he got married. Now both of them are good friends, now they realized their mistake and are now living happily. What I am trying to say here is that love needs understanding, if my friend would have understood her situation and if he would have married her they might be happy together, instead blaming the girl for her mistake would not make love strong, which my friend never did, but life had something else for them in the form of love. Love is always smooth when you drive it, don't complicate love whether it's a boy or girl, when the situation comes fight over situations and make love stable, they should understand each other accordingly instead of utilizing love as an excuse, always consult your parents, they are the stepping stone for love.

Now coming back to my wife's love story, she has a lot of friends and she is very much a shopaholic, her happiness is her hobby in collecting modern ornaments and dress like all other girls. When she was in college, there was a boy who started to follow her whenever she was going to college, and after college initially she never bothered about it, but slowly she started to notice him. They became friends and it continued for one year and this boy all of a sudden proposed to her. She liked him too, but never agreed to accept his love, instead she answered the boy that she would consult with her parents and her sister and tell him the answer. The parents were so nice to her they trusted her for her honesty, so the parents decided to speak with the boy to know whether it was true or not, at that time her father was working abroad and he spoke with the boy about this and came to know that the boy was willing to marry her. So the girl had the confidence to love him right from that day, so with full happiness she accepted his love and they started their love journey. Whenever you ask a boy or girl to describe love, the very first thing which comes to their mind is about their boyfriend or girlfriend, very few talk about their parents. You can hear stories from a person who begins to love, who is in love, who hates love, who is a success in love, who is a flop in love and so on, you can hear a lot. All these happen only when you are in love; there will be no one in this whole planet that has not been in love. Everyone in this world has a lovable heart and a questionable mind, the heart is filled with love and the mind filled with questions, one who knows how to control both and form oneness is what we call a body of love, he has no other qualities other than love, very few possess these qualities and they are very rarely to be found.

Finally my wife started her journey of love as soon as her parents showed her the green signal, but she had two things on her mind, one was whether the boy's parents would accept this marriage, the second one was her elder sister's marriage, both were her problems. She fell in love but her heart stopped working, instead her mind started gossiping. You have a good heart to love, at the same time you need to have a good mind to follow your heart, which none of us does. The heart started to sing the music of love, but the mind kept on disturbing the music of love, like she started to question the boy whether the love would succeed or not. She kept on asking the same question because she never had the confidence in her love, she lost her confidence in her love at the same time the boy was trying to convince her that his parents would accept this marriage when time comes, but she never had that faith. I don't know what made her think so, but she made her mind fixed to that. When you are in love you need to understand and follow what your heart says, the heart never misleads a person, whereas a questionable mind always misleads. If you ask someone to draw the symbol of love, they will a draw a heart-shaped symbol, that's the true symbol of love which denotes love is from the heart. No one will draw a brain symbol for love, even with mentally retarded people, you show them love they will follow you, that is the actual power of love because though the mind wavers, the heart is still felt with love and peace, it does not gossip. You can go only mentally ill, not with your heart, your heart is always be active, full of love, so when you love, love with your heart, it will take you to the right path.

She started to lose her confidence, in love if you don't have confidence then that love will start to fade away, not only in love for that matter, any activity if you don't have the confidence never get into it. I think the boy had the confidence in love, nowadays love is like a thorn, the thorn never finds you and hurts you, accidently it hurts you. If it hurts you just throw it away because no one has the time to bear the pain, or just by applying a medicine you throw that pain away and you just move on, which is far better compared to bearing the pain for a long time. The same applies to love, if at all you are ready to bear the pain then you should have the will to face it, else choose not to bear the pain and find a medicine. My wife belongs to the first category, bear the pain with no confidence, an accident happens in life, it's how you see that accident. I have seen some parents who are against love, obviously they will be against because the tradition, culture, age and the society which we live in, everything differs, that's how they have been brought up, I have heard friends telling me that parents are their enemy in love, never ever blame parents, they are not enemies, they are frightened, the world is moving in advance so they see things which they are not able to accept immediately, but if you give them the hope and if you can convince them that your love can make you happy, obviously they will accept your love. Parents like their children to live happily, that is what they wish for, but your love should give them confidence and not trouble. There are other scenarios where parents accept love, but lovers cannot accept love at some point and then they break up for no reason. So in this the parents are the ones who are suffering. All this is observed by parents themselves, so not to blame them they are in these kind of environments, it's your responsible to make them clear, that's how you see love, and you should try to hold that love for the rest of your life without any complications. Nowadays, parents have started to accept love marriages, it's the people who are in love who are not able to lead it, those days are gone where parents were against love, maybe you can find very few of them somewhere. Whether the marriage is arranged or love it depends how you take love in that marriage.

She never had any complications in getting permission from her parents, it was so easy. There are still some people who follow caste and religion excuses, those days have changed, love has no caste or religion, it's an individual right, that does not mean you can mislead love, instead lead it in the right direction, love will knock your door. Her father was not worried about the caste, all he wanted was his daughter's happiness, so he agreed. She took an oath if at all she married that would be this guy, love made her energetic, love made her strong, love created memories, love created anger, love created happiness, love made her committed, love made her responsible, but she still had the same question raised in her, whether her love would succeed or not. Let's see what made her think so – as soon as she got approval from her parents she asked the boy to get approval from his parents too, for whom he kept on denying, instead he made her convinced in such a way that it started to build a trust in him, so she believed that and continued her journey, but her inner consciousness kept on disturbing her, which she never took seriously. After love, the very next thing is marriage, which makes love the divine commitment. Since her elder sister was not married, she could not rush for her marriage. In India, there is a tradition which is followed – elders get married first, and then the youngest ones, say if there is a boy and girl in a family, no matter whether the girl is elder or younger, the girl will get married first. I don't get what kind of tradition that is, but nowadays, very rarely is this tradition followed, whoever wants to marry first they just do it without any tradition, so her parents said after her elder sisters marriage then comes hers, but her plan was to conduct both of the marriages on the same day, when her elder sister was getting married. This was not possible for her parents since they were not financially capable of it. So they somehow convinced her saying this, but she was not convinced with this, maybe she never believed that her love would be a success one so she couldn't wait for long, so money was the problem for the marriage; the very next step she took seriously was her career. Since her father was working abroad he had to come, and then the rest of the procedures before that. Let's continue with my career where I am still waiting for the contract.

After the interview, three months were already gone, my relatives never trusted me when I said I got selected, so you can imagine what would be their reaction after three months. I better not explain it was worse than expected. I was least bothered about all those, I just sat doing nothing, I was very happy because I liked that. At the same time, I had the confidence that somehow I would get the contract so I never tried for any other job, though everyone asked me to look for some other alternatives. I never troubled my father for money, I did some online jobs and I somehow made money for my living. I am not a person who is greedy for money, if I have I will spend, if not I stay quiet. When I got a spot selected for the interview, there was no evidence to prove that, it was just word of mouth, but I was confident in what they said. I believed them, even though they never gave me any kind of offer letter, but waiting went for more than three months, wherein there was no response from the employer. At the time my parents never believed whether I was telling the truth or not, but my belief continued. I was not at all worried, staying in my house doing nothing, but others who saw me so were very much disturbed. I don't know why, I had even thought 'wow they care for me a lot' but that's not the truth, they were very happy to see me doing nothing because their kids had already been standing at a peak and they didn't want me to become so. But for that purpose, I never wanted to show them, even I can be like that, I never took a chance either. I never was jealous at all in seeing my brothers' growth. I have never, ever thought my life to be a competitive one or result oriented in knowing who is best, no not at all. I will always remain the same whatever turns or twists happen in my life. I had no vision, everyone should live happily with what they have got and never run behind success or money, that's what I believe. What happens when you run behind? Both of these you end up with success and money, but not happiness. When I was in school, there was a teacher who kept on insisting that I had a vision in life, those days I used to visualize sleeping in my home doing nothing, just resting, that's how my vision used to be. Waiting is not wrong, if you know for sure it will happen, so I waited for the contract, so after three months I happened to call the client for the result, which I hated to do because my parents and others compelled. I happened to call the client to know when the contract for the job would reach me. They answered saying that it would take time, till now there was no answer from the employer so I would have to wait for a few days, I had no issue at all hearing this, but my relatives started gossiping about this. I was the one who was directly involved, I myself had no problem but others were so interested in hearing the news. See how strange it is? I don't know why others poke their noses in others' problems when they have their own problems to sort. I personally don't like to get involved in others' personal problems, if at all you get involved then you should solve it smoothly, never create more problems.

Five months since there was no response from the employer. It's very obvious my parents started to blame me, and my relatives started to blame my parents, but I still was not bothered. Whatever happened, I had to face it by my own, so I thought better I face it rather than making it an issue, so I answered everyone who blamed me in a sweet voice that I was very much confident in getting this job. I never gave up, meantime I had a friend of mine who was also waiting to know the result of the interview. For a few of them, though the interview was conducted, they never said the result, instead they asked to wait for a few days to know the result. So one of the guys who kept on buzzing me for the result, I myself didn't know what was going to happen, but I said to him, "never lose hope, instead of calling me, call the employer directly." This guy was very judgmental, he started to think that the employer was fake and he knew very well that I was spot selected, and he was still waiting to know the result. He used to tell me that his final round was so difficult they took forty five minutes, "How come you finished in ten minutes and you are spot selected?" He thought I was not telling the truth, I never tried to explain in detail what happened, I just let him free to say whatever he wanted, by the way he spoke to me I felt that he was jealous. He already had a job, I told him, "You have a job, why should you worry? I don't have a job, I am the one who should be worried but I am not, why do you keep on imagining things before knowing what is going to happen?" and I asked him to wait patiently. Some were eliminated on the spot by the client, only a few were asked to wait, and a few were spot selected, which included me too.

Now coming back to reality, at my stage someone else would have found an alternate job and just moved on, they would not wait like me for one single thing, but my mind never taught me to look for an alternative. My mind was fixed with one job, though I never liked it, I had my mind fixed that job was what I was going to be in. Nowadays, students have different options to find a job, all they need is a computer and the Internet and they will get a job. It has become so easy it's just one touch, even at my time I had those facilities, but I was least interested, my career was not going to decide my life, I am going to decide my life through career. Job gives you happiness only when money flows, if not there is no happiness, according to me happiness should be the job that you do no matter what job it is, but money should not be your happiness. I have friends from school and college who are well settled abroad, whenever they buzz me accidently, I don't have any friends who buzz me sincerely, accidently they do it if I am online so they used to tell I am not happy with the job its very difficult I have heard so many of them telling me the same answer. When you like a job, and if you are happy with what you do, you will never complain, people who complain about their job are not fit to be happy. If you like a job you should be able to cope up with the difficulty as well, when you say it is difficult to do the job, why do you do that job? You can find another alternate job which will make you happy. What is more surprising here is whatever difficulty a guy or a girl is facing in their job, they immediately share those problems either with a friend or family members, which I totally disagree. Why make others skeptical? It's like you making a bad impression on your employer, not only your employer, you yourself, it shows you are lacking in efficiency. There are things which boys and girls should share with parents which they never do at all, instead they gossip a lot. I too faced those kinds of difficulties, but I have thought sharing this difficulty with others will not help you in anyway, all you're doing here is transferring your tension to others who stays without tension. You cannot love your job if you complain, instead do the job that you love, that's what professional ethics is all about. Now you may think anyone can give this kind of advice, it is very difficult to follow; I too agree, but I would definitely say it's easier to follow then to say. Is it difficult to follow the daily routine in your life no right same applies to everything you do. Never love the career, choose the career you love and you will stop complaining.

I have a short sweet story to tell everyone after my college. Initially, I started my career with a multi-national company which was in Chennai, there I had a senior colleague who happened to work there for almost seven years without any interest in the job that he did, though he worked because the girl who he was in love with was also working in the same company. Can you imagine you find these types of people too? I was totally surprised when he said that he was in love with the girl not with the job, he was holding the job for the girl, what surprised me was that the girl didn't even know that this guy was in love with her. Seven years in one job for the sake of a girl, that too I am not worried he served the company for a purpose and the purpose remained a hidden secret. But that inspiration which made him better and better in his job, I have seen him so sincere, punctual, committed and finally dedicated because he followed the footsteps of that girl, the girl who he admired was so perfect in her work, which made him perfect. He started to reach higher levels, and the girl he loved started to notice his growth in that firm so she came to him to congratulate him, she was working for another department in the same company, that was the first day in his life that he spoke to that girl in all those years, can you imagine it? But that is the real fact, so they became friends and this guy got motivated a little, this guy who kept on complaining about the company all the time, who had no interest in his job suddenly started liking the job and the company; he earned happiness in the form of love, he was always happy so he took a courageous decision to propose to her to express his love, so he waited for a day to come to speak with her. The day had finally come, he went with a flower to the desk where she was working and he came out with an upset face and he took a day off and left the office. When going to propose to the girl he was so happy and after that he just left without telling me. I was thinking of the incident all that day, what would have happened? I never had the courage to go and ask the girl about this, even though if I had the courage it would not be fair to interfere in her personal life, so I kept quiet and did my work. A week went by, still this guy never turned up to the office. I tried calling him several times, he was not reachable. So finally I made up my mind to go and ask the girl what really happened; before that, she came to me and asked about the guy. I was shocked, I just thought to do the same, but she herself asked me so I answered her in return, "I was about to ask the same to you, and they said his phone is out of reach, he has not informed the manager either for his leave extension, I don't have any idea what his problem is." When I said this, I looked at her face, her face went reddish and she was so frightened and I asked what really happened, she never wanted to tell me because she never knew that I knew the story, so I told her, "Don't be frightened. I know what happened, you can trust me, and I asked "Did he actually propose to you?" She asked, "Why do you put this question in a doubtful voice?" I told her all these seven years he never had the courage to tell you that he was in love with you, that's why I asked you in some doubt. She said what really happened, the answer is neither yes nor no, but she said she was already married but divorced, "If you are still interested, you can speak with my parents," this is what she said. I never blamed this girl for what she said. Nothing wrong with what she said, that is the fact, but I don't know why this guy was not turning up to the office after this incident, it had already been two weeks, so I thought this guy just left his career and also his love just by hearing this. I know everyone would think the same, boys from the very beginning are always on the cheating side, everyone thinks boys don't take love seriously, but this guy was entirely different. I too never expected this kind of attitude from him. Let me not drag much, three weeks later this guy came with his parents to speak with her parents about their marriage. I was totally out after he said this was why he never returned to the office for three weeks, all these three weeks he convinced his parents and relatives to marry her. You can imagine if a boy who wants to marry a divorced girl, the parents or other members in the family will never agree to it, but my colleague fought for his love because his love was sincere and true, now they are a happily married couple. Boys are not always bad, there are a few boys out there in the world who have a good heart, now you can have so many questions that anyone can review this story in a different angle by giving a negative approach, but what I see here is the situation, the situation makes love stronger, for example, if the girl is married and not divorced then that situation is entirely different, you cannot divert a girl's mind who is already in a relationship, but nowadays that is what is happening outside, which is not fair, at times you have to give up love which makes love stronger, so it all depends how the situation is. So after their marriage his career and his life became very comfortable and happy, the girl made him love his career. You can see different types of people in this world, but very importantly love is the right way to convey your happiness, my point here is, do you think that guy stayed in the company just for the girl he loved? No not at all. He liked what he did, complaining is just an excuse or a hobby just to divert others that he is so hardworking. He loved his career the way he loved his girlfriend, but what he lacked was dedication, that dedication came in the form of a girl.

In my case, I missed dedication because my interests were entirely different, my interests never included career, business or any other work. I was not at all focused, I was focused only on my happiness. It had been five months, I hadn't received the contract yet, I was least bothered, but my parents kept on asking about the contract, not only them my relatives, you know how people react if a guy sitting in his house is doing nothing, obviously they kept on blaming, this continued for a long while and one day everyone kept their mouth shut when the contract finally reached me. Confidence helped me and the people who kept on blaming me never turned up to my house for a long time. So my journey started with a new career and a new beginning. Let's just rewind a little bit and go back to mid school. Do you remember we are still walking? Final examination, final chance to see her, final chance to express my love, final chance to show my courage and finally is your expectation, what happens?

An interesting fact, which I would like to share when I think about the final examination, tenth board exams, I know everyone in their life will remember these board exams which come first in your life and which is your first step in your career life. Tenth board exams are so important in each and every one's life, this incident happened when I was in tenth grade. I call this period a vacation period, this is the only time you will get a lot of study leave. I hope everyone agrees with it, study leave is to sincerely sit in an individual's house and study those who have friends, they do group studies, those who want to do combined studies they do that, but do you think they study? No, not at all, they do only last minute studies. I fall in that category, let me come to the incident, it was during study leave, our accounts teacher was a very sincere teacher since she wanted her students to score good marks in accounts, she kept two to three hours accounts class during all study leave so it became a compulsion for the whole class to attend it. I had three other friends who accompanied me to my house after the special class. Once the class was over, we used to go to a hotel to have tea which would be so good during cold season. One day these guys planned to take me to a nearby forest and show me the ghost, they knew very well I was so frightened and I didn't go to places which are frightening, so these guys planned it but they never told me, instead they said they wanted to show me one place where we could do group studies, because the place was so calm and quiet I too agreed. Next day, after special class as usual we had our regular tea and these guys took me to a place which was full of trees, rather than calling it a place you could call it a forest; the weather condition was so cloudy and misty on that day and very cold too, these guys opened their books and kept on studying seriously so I thought these guys were taking me somewhere to seriously study for the board exams. So I took a book from my bag and kept on reading, there was a lot walking and it was so silent in there, no one was there except us and finally we reached a locked bungalow. It was so huge and beautiful it looked like a ghost house, these guys tried and looked through the window and I asked, "What are you guys looking at so seriously?" They said in a very low voice, "There is a ghost here, we have seen it here several times." I asked them what, again they repeated saying there was a ghost. So they asked me to look in through the window for me to believe. I was frightened because I lacked courage to speak in front of everyone, that was my only fear, but I was not frightened of anything else, particularly ghosts. I don't believe that they even exist, so I looked in through the window of the house and I was stunned, not frightened, just stunned seeing a woman walking inside the house wearing a white sari in a locked bungalow. I couldn't believe my eyes, my friends thought that it was a ghost, but it was difficult for me to believe so. After some time the woman disappeared and we were never able to find her inside the house; we waited there for sometime to check whether we would be able to see her, once again as suspected, we saw the woman inside the house in the same costume. We were not able to find the truth hidden in that house, so we went back to our house, but my mind was thinking, why would a woman be inside a locked house wearing a ghost costume? You know we imagine ghosts are always in white costumes, the reason is the media have given an idea this is how a ghost would be dressed; it was hard for me to believe but my friends believed that was the ghost. The mystery continued for days, so we planned to visit the house once again to make it clear, so we once again went inside the forest and looked through the window of the house to see the same woman, if she was real or a fake ghost. Now through that window we were able to see two women walking with white costumes, and there were some strange noises in that house. It was like a ghost visual treat for me, my friends were so frightened, but I was so happy to see live ghosts walking. My doubt was why were these woman walking in the same room when they had another room, it remained suspicious for me, they never frightened us either. My friends started to debate on this topic, whether they were real ghosts or fake; everyone agreed that they were real except me. So I said to my friends, "We have seen ghosts frightening people, for a change let's frighten ghosts." No one agreed to my plan but my mind kept on telling me that I somehow should do that. So I took a stone and threw it at the window and ran away. I heard the window's glass break and we just ran without noticing anything, later that night I had a dream of that woman walking in my room, so I never took it seriously because it was just a dream; whenever your mind is attracted to one thing very deep, as you go deeper it will reflect in your dream, so that dream was just a reflection of my thoughts. So after that incident we never went to visit that place; once again we had our tenth board exams and on our last day of our final we friends once again decided to visit the place. This time my friend had a camera with him to take a photo of the ghost so we went to that place once again; the window which was broken was fixed, the bungalow was painted and there was a family at this time, so we thought let's go back, but I thought it's better to go to that family and say what we saw there. My friends disagreed, but I went towards them and saw inside the house that there were two women walking inside with the same costume; I was not shocked this time, instead I wanted to ask why did they keep on walking like that? There was a man who was dressed up like a doctor coming out of that house and he asked me, "Who are you and what do you want?" So I explained to him from the beginning what happened all these days. The man started laughing and said, "Those are my twin sisters who are not mentally fit," and he also said that he and his wife were doctors, most of the time they were out so they used to lock the door and go. I knew for sure this would end up something like this, but my friends created stories. With this I apologized to the doctor for what happened and came back. This was a very funny incident which happened during my tenth board exams, there are no such things called ghosts, they don't really exist, we create them.

Coming back to mid school, I was walking behind her and she was walking with my friend. It was a partial rainy and a sunny day, what is the first thing that comes to our mind for partial weather like this? At that mid school age kids are all attracted to see a colorful rainbow, I was walking looking at the rainbow, it was so colorful, bright and beautiful, our life is also colorful like that but we don't make it colorful, so the rainbow was a motivational factor for me at that time. At the same time my friend was looking at me and me showing signs not to come near her and speak to her, which made me a little upset and also frightened. Now the dream which I saw was almost becoming true, the visuals which I had in my dream differ but the atmosphere is the same. So we reached our school and we finished our exams, it was time to say goodbye to each other so I thought this would be the right time to speak with her. So I waited for my turn to say goodbye to her, as I was waiting my friend came near me to say goodbye and also said that he proposed to the girl and he continued telling me stories about what really happened. I was not listening to his stories, what I wanted to know from him was what was her reaction, but he never said that, all he said was that he expressed his love, now the dream became reality, I was not bothered whether he was in love or she was in love, all I was worried about was what the term love actually means. You know at that age you can see love as friendship nothing more, so I was in some confusion, what was I lacking here? Was it because I was not talking to anyone, was it because I was not acting funny in front of others, was it because I was not good looking? All these were running in my mind. Was this love? I had no idea. I knew I was attracted to her, but what was that attraction trying to do here? Was it making me jealous? Was it making me playful? Was it making me inactive? There were lot of questions which were running in my mind, an age where you cannot define love, but still we call it love. So I waited for my chance to say goodbye to her, and I also made up my mind to ask her about the incident that my friend kept on telling with so much anxiety. So I went near her, those days in mid school students had a system to say goodbye in a different style, they said goodbye by wrinkling ink through ink pen in our dress, that is how they used to say goodbye with happiness, so everyone of them was doing it, except I never wanted to do this but everyone else wrinkled ink at me. When I went to her she smiled at me and said, "See here, the loser is here in front of us," and called her friends and insulted me in front of them. I felt so bad and embarrassed, but never gave up, she kept on insulting me with her friends but I took that in a sportive way and I said to her that I would like to speak with her personally, but she never agreed. So in front of the others I once again said "I love you," but this time she called my friend and informed, "He is telling me the same thing what you said to me a little while ago." I never had a question to ask her about the incident, what my friend said, she made it clear, now I was frightened to face him. My friend looked at me very angrily, in front of everyone he slapped me. I never knew why he did that. Was it just because I said 'I love you' to her? Everyone started laughing at me which made my friend so proud in that situation. I never cried, instead I asked him "You said the same love to your uncle's daughter, just tell me the difference between that love and this love." He gave me another slap and they just walked without saying goodbye to me. I never liked it so I called them and wished every one of them a happy holiday and a sweet goodbye; once again she turned back and gave me a cute smile which made me happy and to forget the incident. At that age love is playful and eagerness grows in you in such a way that if a friend comes and tells you that he is also in love with the same girl, there is eagerness to know whether she accepted it or not, because you don't trust girls. From a girl's point of view she is innocent at that age, she gets attracted to boys who are talkative and who impresses her, but she accepts love thinking that love is just a game of attraction. That's what the girl here did, she felt that the boy impressed her in so many ways, that I was not that impressive. So my mid school love ended up there with a funny incident, but life had another twist. My mid school life ended there and I had to switch over to another school, meanwhile my parents were looking in for schools for my admission.

When I say admission here, I am reminded about an incident which happened when I completed my twelfth grade and was thinking about what to do next, at that time I happened to travel to different colleges to know about the courses they offered, I personally never had any interests in choosing a subject, all I wanted to do was something which was easy to learn without any difficulty. There was a guy who was staying near my house who did hotel management, who always used to tell me, "This course is very easy, the course deals with practical exams rather than theoretical exams," which made me think about that course, so I decided to take a subject something like that, it was not my personal interest to take up a course which was beneficial in future. I never thought about future benefits, all I thought was easy to learn, so I expressed my interest to my parents and they agreed, so I thought it would be better if we went personally to college and enquired about the cost involved for this course and its duration. So my grandfather accompanied me to travel to colleges to enquire about the course. My grandfather used to tell me, "Why do you want to go and study leaving your parents, instead you can choose a college here and take some course which is easy." What he said was good, but the colleges which offered this course were cost effective so my father never had that much money for an admission there so I had to search other colleges. I explained this to my grandfather. So we started to travel in a bus, it would take around three hours from my place to our destination, we were sitting in the bus, just before us there was a couple sitting, my grandfather very rarely sleeps when travelling, nor did I, as we were travelling the couple who were sitting in front of us were disturbing others by talking loud and doing some stupid actions, altogether the behavior was not tolerable, which my grandfather never liked. There are some people who react to social nuisance, my grandfather falls under that category, if he sees something wrong he immediately reacts to it. So by seeing this couple's action, he just couldn't tolerate and asked them, "Are you all married?" The guy in return asked, "What is your problem?" The scenario changed and everyone started to stare instead of stopping the fight, I pulled my grandfather to stop fighting several time but he never stopped, according to my grandfather what they were doing was wrong and he had a point, because they were just college students. So he just asked them not disturb others, but the guy behaved very badly, he wanted to act as man in front of his girl so he too never gave up, finally the bus conductor came and stopped the fight, and they never continued with the actions after that. Very rarely you find people who react to these kind of situations, though they were lovers love is not to disturb others in public, some people stare at these people for fun, some react to it, my question here is, why do they spoil the public in the name of love? Finally we reached our destination and we went inside a college to enquire about the course, the college was moderate and the atmosphere was good, the cost was much better and as we walked in the college campus you could see girls and boys sitting and chatting, some were hugging, some were holding their hands and so on, my grandfather immediately said, "You don't need this college, this college does not have the college atmosphere, he couldn't tolerate all this, obviously the generation had changed so I made him understand what the reality was. This would be the scenario in the rest of the college as well, it's one's view how to handle the situation, see what is required in life and leave the rest to God, that's what he kept on telling me every time, so I shared the same dialogue to him at that time. He is a true believer in God not me, the world is like that, we cannot change the world, all we can do is close our eyes, see things which are good, never take these kind of visuals seriously. But he was not convinced, the real fact is wherever you see you can spot a lover, that's how the society is, love is good. I don't blame but that love shouldn't be a disturbance to others. You can react to people who take it seriously, but not to people who don't know the meaning of respect and don't listen to a person who is trying to make them understand what is good for them, and if you go on reacting to it you will have only time for that. Somehow I finalized a college for my admission.

High school, the place where I realized a lot about life, initially when I got an admission in a convent school I was a bit frightened that time because language and the English accent was difficult to follow, so at the beginning stage it was very difficult for me to cope up with everyone. My father was very adamant in getting his kids into English medium school and that too in a school where Indians were very rare, so it became a compulsion for me to learn and communicate only in English. So I had no choice to skip communication, when

I was in mid school it was an easy task to communicate with teachers in our mother tongue as well as known language, but in high school that was not possible. So I maintained absolute silence, when I entered the new school I followed the same silence as when I was in mid school, no friends, no activities or games, no extra curricular activities, nothing, but I studied well, where I managed to hold first or second rank I never gave up in studies. It was entirely a different experience from the previous school that I was in, in my previous no one voluntarily came and spoke to me either, in this school everyone tried to be friends with me, but I was not interested in making friends. So I just did my work, I joined the school during my sixth grade and till ninth grade I never had any friends, or I never participated in anything. I travelled in my fantasy world where no one disturbed me, which I liked very much. I have heard children who are very naughty, some may be very intelligent, some are average, I never fell in any of these category I remained silent. It is almost five kilometers from my house to school so the school had arranged a school busy for small children, those days I hated to travel in the school bus, you would not get a seat to sit, it would be so crowded. I used to puke in the bus all the time, for almost three years I never stopped puking so as I got into the bus, if I didn't get a window seat I would puke. So whenever I got into the bus there would be a window seat reserved for me because everyone was frightened of me because if I puked the whole bus would start to smell, wherein others also would puke so they never took that risk. Everyone hated to speak with me, even in the bus; there was a girl in the bus who used to call me puke face all the time, I never bothered.

Teachers as well as professors have tried their level best to make me participate in sports, debates, quiz and singing competitions, but I never participated in anything, but I was a rank holder, in that school if you took first or second rank they used to appreciate it by giving a rank holder badge wherein you continued to wear it from sixth grade till ninth grade. When I was in ninth grade my attitude started to change. I personally wanted to do something different from the others, but my fear always stopped me from participating in any competition. Usually in all schools after tenth grade students have an option to choose a group in which you would like to continue the rest of the years, but this school had this choice in ninth grade itself, as usual I never took the science group, I didn't like science. Instead I took the commerce group though I never liked it, I like one single subject which was accounts. I did well in studies as always but my mind never allowed me to participate in any other competition because of my fear, when everyone bunked classes saying that they had sports practice, this practice, that practice, I used sit in class and study, which I slowly started to hate. In class I always used to dream for nothing, I was totally a daydreamer, one of the girls from my class noticed this and she started to make fun of me by a nickname "brahmae" which is daydreamer in Tamil. This name started to spread among each and everyone in the school, as a matter of fact even teachers and professors started to make fun of me with that name. I am a person who takes everything sportive so I never minded them calling me in that name. This girl who kept this name had a crush on me, I don't know what made her like me, but she always used to tell me that she liked me the way I was in the class. At that time, I never took that crush seriously because within quotes she said she liked me the way I was in class, which meant she never liked me. That's how I thought, so I never took it seriously. But the nickname she gave spread so fast I was known to the whole school within months, till then no one was aware or noticed that this person is studying in the school, though I was a rank holder I was not that famous, but the name made me famous within months. The credit goes to the school, I personally thanked her for making me famous, she too never expected that which made her cozy and also hate me because she never liked me being famous. Ego started to grow in me.

When I say ego, I would like to share a short story, when do you think ego starts to grow on you? From the time you were born as you grow it grows in you. If it doesn't grow then you are a superhero, before that what do you actually mean by EGO? Don't search for a dictionary I will tell you, your ego is your conscious mind, the part of your identity that you consider your "self," if you say someone has a big ego then you are saying he is "full of himself," which is very dangerous, not only dangerous, it's a poison, there is no medicine for it, you have to cure it yourself. Let me come back to the story, this happened when I was in eighth grade, at that time I had a passion on a cycle, I was so crazy to ride a cycle, usually kids at that age are very much attracted to cycles, kids have passions at different ages, but me being a kid that was my first passion towards a cycle. I had a cousin brother who already had a cycle, but never had a chance to borrow or to ride the cycle, for that fact, who gives to share their own things? Ego is the main reason which will not allow things to be shared. My father was not financially sound at that time but I never thought that my ego never allowed me stay in my house, by seeing a cycle which my cousin brother had, so I kept on torturing my father to buy me a cycle, so finally he bought me a cycle. Do you think ego stopped there? No, never, as months passed I wanted a big cycle and my father bought me a better one, my cousin brother seeing this he couldn't sleep, he too wanted a big cycle, each one's ego never let us free, it started from a cycle and from thereon for each and everything competition started, ego is very dangerous if you don't know how to control and handle it. This is just the beginning of ego in you. I just gave you a small sample of it, this is not only for children, it applies to adults as well, as adults ego is very much natural in society that we are termed egoistic. Ego is not a character it is natural, but one should know not to be it. In simple, if an individual gets jealous of another individual's growth which makes him upset and not happy, that's his ego, at the same time if he is happy with all his heart then he is a superhero, you may think why is he saying superhero all the time? I call enlightened masters as superheroes.

My fame started when I was in ninth grade unexpectedly, now my instincts started questioning me, I should overcome my fear and be very active like others, for that I needed a platform which I had now so I took this chance. So as days moved, the boy who was silent started to become very naughty, which surprised my parents and friends.

A short story of a friend of mine, this guy was born and bought up in Bangalore, he had no parents, he studied staying with his uncle and soon after his graduation he got a good job in one of the top most multi-national companies in India. Once me and my friends went to Bangalore for a tour, we happened to meet and then we became friends, this guy is very intelligent and a smart worker. I have never seen a person like that who is so much dedicated in his work, he was so sincere and dedicated. He had offers from top companies, he had visited many other countries and he received so many awards and certification for his outstanding performance. His uncle was so proud of him and everything was going on fine until a girl entered his life. Nowadays, corporate companies don't encourage an individual to grow in their company because each individual is jealous of the other's growth, it's a competitive world where everyone fights for his own survival, don't have time to care for others, everyone single one of them wants to be famous overnight. But for my friend, he never ran behind fame, his dedication towards his work brought fame which others never liked. Private sectors are not like government sectors they have a different package system, according to the private sector performance matters, if a guy performs well he is given a hike in his earning package every year. My friend was getting a hike continuously, this guy is very innocent he never complains of his work or gets tiresome of his work twenty four seven he is engaged with his work. When a girl entered his life, his job lacked dedication, she too was in the same company where he worked, but this girl was not that dedicated in her work. Love has its own set of rules and the company has another set of rules, he got messed up with these two rules, love needs dedication rather than dedication it needs more understanding, but the company needs only dedication. When they started their relationship, everything went on fine, when they dived in deeper, the girl started complaining saying "He never calls me frequently, he never has time to spent with me, he never memorizes my birthday," and she had a long complaint list, in which the guy was trapped. The guy started to lack dedication in work and started to show his dedication in love because he was fed up of the girl who kept on complaining. All these years fame was following him but now he started to follow it, but with his problems he started losing it. This guy started to realize that the company started to have a bad impression on his performance. So one day he was thrown out of that company because he lacked in his attendance and constant performance, as I said in the beginning the private sector needs only performance, survival in a company is totally based on performance. The girl started to notice his failure, so she also slowly started to break up the relationship which the boy began to realize very lately. Now he was left alone, when he lost everything he started to realize his mistakes, he never fought with the girl or the company, he just maintained silence. He accepted and realized his own mistake so there were no issues, which is one thing which I liked in him, if he would have thought he could have made the scenario worse, but what is the point? There will be no solution, though it made him a little upset, he never gave and continued his life. The mistake was from both of them, the girl was not in love, was behind his fame, the boy was not behind fame, was behind of love but both never worked out. Fame should follow you and if by chance you get it, try not to spoil it and don't be behind it. The boy and the girl never knew what love was. In the name of love the boy lost his career, and in the name of love the girl cheated on him, both were equally wrong. When you do something with dedication, do that alone with oneness, never mix it with others else you will lose that oneness spirit. You may think, what would have happened to that girl and boy after that incident, life had something else for them, but they were not together after that, the girl married another guy and got a divorce within years, and the boy got married and lived happily. Fame is just an excuse, love never depends on fame.

Instead, sticking with the word famous, let's continue with popularity. I think popularity is the right word to use, high school has earned me popularity just by a nickname, which earned me friends, courage, communication, love, anger, greed, education, humor, relationship and most importantly a bad name. I started experiencing a new life full of fun and enjoyment, a guy who never made friends began to make end numbers of friends. The girl who made me popular in school never admired me after that, I too never bothered. If you ask someone in schooldays "have you ever fell in love or have you ever had a crush in school, ninety five percent of them would say yes," for that fact you don't have to be in mixed school, there are boys who get attracted to girls even though parents put them in boys' higher secondary school. I am not motivating love here, that's how the world is, we cannot blame boys or girls for this fact at that age we get attracted, but we make a mistake calling it love, love cannot be defined at that age. Do you think parents have time to look each and every time at what their kids are up to? I agree it's not possible, but they can spend some time with them to understand them. Kids at some age are very naughty, but parents should know how to handle them in a smooth way, which most of the parents don't do. Attraction at school age cannot be stopped, that's how humans are, it is very natural, now coming back to reality – as parents we know kids are going to school and we believe our kids do only good things, or we believe our kids will never do anything without our knowledge, which is absolutely wrong, give them the freedom but make sure you follow what their freedom is all about. When you move into cities, towns, villages you can see so many boys and girls, do you know how safe and secure they are? We don't know right, so parents should spend maximum time with their kids at all stages till they realize what life is, else kids commit mistakes and we put the blame on them.

Let me continue with my school life, I too had attraction in my schooldays, I too called that attraction love. When I was in ninth grade I started to form a crush with a girl who is senior most, it was just an attraction, in schooldays, if you have a crush the very next thing you do is share it with your friends verbally, you didn't have social networks those days to share it publically, nowadays sharing has become so easy via social networks, I have seen friends who are always online from the day begins till the day ends, when I say social network I am reminded about a short incident which happened recently, you have so many social networks but Facebook is one networking site which the majority of my friends use. People started to share and update facts in social media; it has its own advantage and disadvantage. Those who know that will utilize social networking sites in a proper way; technology is good, we make it bad, so people who don't know how to utilize they make social media a mess. My friend signed up with a social network site with a mindset to make new friends; people who enter into these kinds of sites, especially boys create a lot of fake accounts, which my friend was aware of. So as soon as he signed up, within days he made so many friends, obviously boys looking for girls, so he made a lot of friends. He became very close to a girl and began a wide relationship with her. But he never had a chance to speak with her over the phone, they continued conversing through online buzz. This online relationship became strong so one day this guy wanted to meet this girl face to face. So the guy decided to meet in the girl's place where she stayed, so this guy packed up and got ready to travel to the north from the south with the excitement to see her. Finally he reached the destination, as soon as he reached there he gave a buzz online stating that he had reached the destination, but the place she mentioned never existed. He tried to contact her online but there was no response, the account was offline. He waited there for one week and came back to his place with a flop face, when he reached his place, he tried to look in online once again and she was online and this is what she mentioned, "I was out of station when you came here, can you come once again?" but the boy said goodbye to the relationship and deleted his profile. I know you have so many questions in your mind, that was a fake account with some celebrity photo, could not identify whether it was a he or she, but was known by a girl name, she played with the boy's emotions, but the boy realized his stupid mistake when friends advised him. He thought love was true so he did something stupid, but he realized his mistake so he never made it an issue, as far as I know he never used any other social networking sites after that incident. Nowadays, everyone is swimming in these sites, sharing things which are not required, creating problems, making strangers as friends and sharing things with strangers, this is what is happening in this world. My friends used to tell a phrase which they frequently used after Facebook came into existence, which is "keep me posted." Don't forget to keep your life also posted.

So I shared my crush with my friends, I never felt love within, it was just an attraction, but friends made this complicated, each one had different opinions, some said it was love, some said it was infatuation, so friends started to twist the relationship, so they provoked me to express the crush to the girl. But I was not interested in expressing, rather I liked to admire her but friends never let me admire, instead they kept on compelling me to propose to the girl. Sometimes you happened to get trapped by what a friend says, because you don't realize the consequences. But I never fell in that trap, instead I waited for a day to express my love, and instead I informed them I would express my love when I felt so, after that they never disturbed me, asking to propose to the girl. Friends at a certain age play a vital role in our life, especially during school and colleges, once you enter your career life then there is no time to spend some time with them, but now, since the technology changed everyone stays with friends online all the time. Mobiles, Internet, social networks made life easy to new generations to learn a lot of things then there, but it all depends on the way an individual utilizes the modern technology. For some, friends act as a twist in one's life, for some it is just the opposite, I fall under the second category.

Friends, there are a few friends who will be there to help you when you are in trouble, there are a few other friends who will not poke their nose in any trouble, you can trust them, but there are a few others who stay in the center with a suspense, you cannot trust them. Till my ninth grade I never had many friends, but after that I earned a lot, but no one stayed for long, there are people who categorize friends as good, bad, best which I don't like, a friend is always a friend. There is no good, bad or best friend. I have personally experienced right from my mid school till college among friends there will be a group and among that group there will be categorization like best friends, so what about others, they are not best. When you take social networking sites, friends are classified as mutual friends, we create this categorization which is not healthy, everyone of them are best, even when you take social networks there is a separate department for mutual, mostly all of my friends who are in these kind of sites dive in these sites maximum, in search of friends from school and colleges, and there are few who sign up only to search girls. I too have experienced these so-called social networking sites, but very lately just to know what it really means, but I am least interested to dive there for twenty four hours and keep on updating each and every second of your life's moments. Posting photos for others to see, you know social networks turned out to be a fantasy world. My point here, friends should not be categorized, everyone is the same, the reason is when you categorize love is not visible, it becomes invisible. There is a short story behind this observation, when I was in eighth; a time when I never joined any group of friends, at that there was a group of three friends, I also used to stay with them, even though I didn't speak much I usually spent my break and lunchtime with them. In this group we had a friend who was different from the others, he looked like Mr. Bean, a great comedy artist who acts in Hollywood movies, he was similar to that artist, he was funniest among us in the class, his actions and behavior was the same as the comedian artist, so everyone used to make fun of him calling him Mr. Bean. This guy was in the same group, so altogether we were four, among these four there were two best friends who were always together all the time, they support each other in tests, exams, their friendship was so astonishing, I was not at all bothered. I just went with them when I was free, but the other guy used to go with the best friends wherever they went, but these best friends had their rules so they kept on avoiding this guy, no one else used to talk with this, this guy was alone all the time, but the whole class used to make fun of him when he showed some action, he never used to mind, but he used to tell me all the time, "None of the girls are talking to me, everyone has best friends but I don't have any." He knew me very well, that I didn't encourage someone who came and told me to become his or her best friend, so he never asked me to become his best friend, but he needed someone who took special care but no one was interested. The whole year went very quick but till the end this guy never had a best friend, you know why friends need best friends, they believe that best friends are always trustworthy.

I don't agree with that, everyone is trustworthy, it's because we choose friends who are the best to our knowledge, we don't choose everyone as the best. After that year he left the school for this reason. I don't understand why people categorize people. We don't mention there is a group of best friends standing; we always mention there is a group of friends standing, never criticize others. We don't have the rights to judge who is best so follow that everyone is best.

Once you know for sure that you are going to get settled in one job, the very next thing you think about is marriage, you start to dream about your life partner and so on. I too, started to think about marriage that's not because I am settled, when I started to feel absolute loneliness, I thought I needed someone who takes real care of my parents and who understands what love is and teaches me love. I never had any imaginations that my life partner should be like this or like that at all, I needed someone who loved me like my mother did when I was a baby. There were a few elders who advised me that at a certain age we tend to lose our virginity, so automatically we tend to see some changes in our hormones, so it is better to get married at a certain age. When they said at that time I couldn't understand it, but I realized what they were trying to tell me. According to me marriage never depends on sex, though it is an important factor in life, it is just a part of life, there is life beyond sex, as humans we are a bond of sex it is quite natural, when you say lovemaking obviously it is again sex, but ninety five percent of our people don't know the real meaning of sex, they use the word love for sex, this is what everyone does. Love and sex are two different things, never mix love with sex, love itself takes time, so you can imagine how much time it takes to do lovemaking. It is beyond love, I have come across people who ignore love just for this reason, which I don't agree, if there is love, sex follows automatically, that's what we call lovemaking, lovemaking is not just sexual pleasure, it still differs from people to people, according to me it is understanding, patience, emotions, love, care, happiness, there are so many qualities and after all this then comes what we say sex into existence, if you don't follow the qualities in love, and if you follow only sex then that is not true love, that is just pleasure. So married life includes as said, losing your virginity like in a flower, a flower loses its virginity as soon as it blossoms till then it never show its beauty, once it shows its beauty it loses its virginity, the same with clouds, clouds try to cover the virginity of the sky, when the clouds are cleared then you can enjoy the virginity of a clear sky. Likewise sex too has its own virginity, as per Indian culture, marriage acts as an open sky and a flower to know the beauty in sexual relationship. Married life totally depends on how the relationship is weighed in terms of love and sex. Nowadays, sex has become an open relationship, wherever you turn you can see this, it has become a nuisance to the public, in parks, beach, theaters, malls, stations, you cannot go out with your family, no one can stop, small children who see this try to grab all this in their minds and the generations become worse, where is this world going? They do all this in the name of love, I don't understand why they term this love when they don't know what love is.

Love has become a hobby nowadays, since the technology is well advanced it has become more easy, how many stories do we hear each and everyday, does this not have an end? Obviously until and unless each individual realizes this. Let's hope that day will come soon. I don't blame people who love, but that love shouldn't be a burden to others, if one can realize this then no one will commit a mistake. India is known for its divine culture, let that culture remain the same, that's India's beauty. Let's dream for a better India which is in the hands of younger generations like us. Love is unstoppable I agree, but sex and rape in the name of love is stoppable. Let's just not get diverted here, it's just a small message which I wanted to convey. Let's get back to my married life.

We say marriages are made in heaven. On what basis do we say this phrase, does anyone have any idea how heaven looks like or anyone who has travelled to heaven shared any experience? Heaven is just an imaginary world, heaven and hell is where we are, there is no such world, the world we live in is heaven as well as hell, we created it. Yes marriages are made in heaven we live in; heaven is our own Mother Earth. I still remember my grandfather used to tell me, "My son, the activities which we do here whether it is good or bad in earth has been calculated, if you do good you go to heaven after death, if you do bad you go to hell after our death, in that case none of us in this world goes to heaven." When you stay with grandparents you can actually learn a lot of things, whether you believe them or not it sounds good to be an interesting fact. My grandfather is a religious person, he used to advise me a lot and tell a lot of stories, though I don't believe I liked to hear the facts which he always used to tell me. I used to ask him who calculates all this good and bad in us, he used to tell me God calculates, so I asked him, God does not have any other work apart from this? He is actually trying to create a fear in me not to do anything bad, older generations have the habit to teach their grandchildren, telling these kinds of stories, without them you actually don't even know whether there was a character called God. They are the ones who specialized in telling religious stories, if you take the new generation, who is ready to listen to those kind of stories, to be frank religious stories are a fantasy, those days superheroes are religious heroes. Olden days, if you asked a kid who is your superhero he would tell you Lord Krishna, Lord Jesus, Lord Ram, Lord Siva, Allah and so on, at the same time if you ask the new generation they will tell you, Hitman, Superman, Batman, Spiderman and so imagine the generation gap. Nowadays, who likes to hear stories none of us are interested to know facts which are useful, none of them have the time. My grandfather had his own set of rules, to be precise he is a time follower, he does everything in time from the start of the day till he finishes all his work, he needs to get his intake in time, if not he will not accept, he was not strict but everyone thought that he was strict. No one actually liked him since he was religious, he is not modernized, when his children grew up and got well settled, their lifestyle changed wherein they never liked the way he lived his life. He had his own way of dressing, and most importantly he was very fond of kids. I loved him for what he was but at some point I was not able to be with him during his time of his death, which I regret even now. Before that I was so close to him, he liked me a lot, I had a chance to spend some point of my life with my grandparents, which is really a gift on earth. I have observed fights in the family, not only in my family, almost all family, when parents become old they turn out to be burden to their own kids, you actually need them till they give you good education and once you get settled you forget them. How many of you all actually live for your parents? I don't blame everyone on this fact but mostly none live for their parents. I would like to narrate a story which my friend said, the story is about my friend who stayed in a joint family, when you take family there are people who stay away from parents, some stay with parents; some are joint family and so on.

This guy was talking about the life's difficulty in a joint family, he was the youngest of all in his family, the family consisted of two elder sisters and two brothers, and they were very rich so their parents never had the difficulty in giving them all a good education and a good life, everyone got well settled in their stream. So one day their parents had a huge loss in their business, which they did and their parents suffered a lot and finally they were in a stage to sell all their properties to overcome their loss, this is the time life teaches you what life actually needs when you stand alone, when parents were left alone kids started to avoid them, happiness in their family started to fade away, now there was a fight among their kids who will look after their parents. Till then parents believed that their kids would be there for them all the time, but they were wrong, when they had money they got that respect, when they lost money they lost their respect too. Finally, parents had to stay in my friend's elder brother's house and they were treated worse by the elder brother's wife, but they adjusted well without any fight because they were left without any other options, they had to survive. I still remember one thing which my friend said, when parents have assets everyone equally fights for the asset, equally when it comes to the life of their own parents no one has the same equality. When you are happy, if you have a chance to share the same happiness with your family, your grandparents and others, it's a great gift. What is the point praising God if you don't praise your own parents? My grandfather used to say this frequently, which is one thing I liked in him the most. Though I never believed in God I agree to what he says, the living gods are our parents, there are people who spend money visiting temples and demand of God for a good life, on the other hand they treat their parents very badly. What is the point giving to God when you don't give it your parents, I have never come across parents who demand money from their kids, they are happy with what they get, the other thing which my grandfather taught me was at the time you were born you come to this world of hope so bring nothing, the hope continues till your life reaches a climax so you take nothing, during the period of your lifetime you earn a lot of assets, friends, relatives, love so on, but are you sure you earned a good name? That's what hope is all about, he reminded me of this every time, hope is not earning money or assets in life, hope is earning a good name which makes others remember you even after your death, so you are still alive in others' hearts in the form of love. Change your attitude towards hope and start living with a hope to help, love, secure others.

I got married at the age of twenty eight, love has no age, but love differs at each age, obviously there is a certain age to get married, you can't marry at the age you think, in our country there are certain rules which have to be followed, if a person thinks that he is ready to secure a girl life that is the right time to get married, for a guy this maturity level is attained only after twenty five years, till then he will have no idea what love and life is are, for some it may take even more, according to girls' maturity, growth is very fast compared to boys, that doesn't mean that they can get married at the age before eighteen, for girls after the completion of eighteen is a good age to get married, but nowadays girls too have ideas to get married only when they think that they are well settled in life. During my grandfather's period child marriage was in its peak. Marriage totally depends on love, but we categorize marriage in three different ways love, arranged and register marriage, but in all these love remains the same, but it has different stages, stages here is the duration of love. Love plays a vital role only in love marriage; though love is involved in arranged marriage it takes a long time, in simple if love is successful that becomes a love cum arranged marriage, if not that turns out to be a register marriage. Mine was an arranged marriage, and I got married at the right age, but marriage had something else for me in return, before that let me continue with my career from where I stopped.

As I said in the beginning, after my graduation I kept on fluctuating, as far as I know I stayed in one company for a long while when I went abroad, till then I kept on fluctuating but I never stayed in my house without any work. I did something or the other, but nothing gave me pure satisfaction. After moving into so many companies I finally decided to go abroad, when I got my contract for the sake of my parents, the contract clearly stated that I had to stay in that company for two years, and there was a bond, which made me a little upset, but somehow I managed to fly abroad. Relatives and friends were shocked thinking that how come this guy got a chance to fly, some said that's his luck, some said going abroad was not a big deal, some said the job sounds average, some said he has no other work he will come back within months, there were so many opinions but my parents it's God's grace, I never listened to anyone, I thought it's the companies fate that a person like me is going to work with them. First time you experiencing a flight journey, I had a friend who accompanied me during my journey, he was so excited to travel on the flight because that was his first time, even me too. Everything from ticket fare, visa, food was taken care of by the employer, we never paid even a single penny, either for consultancy or travel agents, it was totally taken care by the employer, which is what shocked my relatives. I have never come across anyone, whether my family or friends, who motivated others when they did something good except my grandfather. I always never had a passion to work, to be frank I don't know what my passion is all about. So me and my friend started our first journey in flight, he was so keen to take the window seat, I too never fought for the window seat either, if you look at his body you will not fight with him that's how he is, usually people fight with people who are below average than them because they know for sure he cannot beat them in return, some people get angry soon, they react immediately, those kind of people when it comes to work, the manager will be shouting at them for not doing their work, within him he is very angry but he will not show it to him, if he does he will be fired, so they wait patiently, once the manager finishes, the guy goes out, he is already frustrated, he somehow has to release his frustration so at that time maybe he will get a call from his girlfriend or wife, so he takes that chance to show his frustration to them, so it continues from person to person, finally it ends up with so many troubles and you call that day is not my day. The same applies to a woman, well not only a man does this, even women, if you have kids that's it, then that kid is dead. I have seen it often in almost all companies as well as in families, instead of all these complications, if you stay mum accepting your mistake you will never have this kind of trouble, then and there your frustration is solved, but how many of them do that? Only very few.

So my friend kept on talking which I never liked, he was boasting over his previous employers and about his education and so, I hate people who boast, they are not creators. I had no other choice other than listening to him, at the time of take off this guy tried to make me frightened by transferring his negative energy to me, explaining about the consequences and accidents, he tried to act that he knew everything about the flight and he also mentioned that he worked in an airport as a customer service agent for a while. I am a person who is always positive, his stories never made me frightened but I silently listened to him because I didn't want to hurt him either, so I always smiled. There are people like this who always have such a negative attitude, but they never stop there, they pass the same energy to others as well which will create more fear, there are people who are even frightened of silly things, you cannot change them, but they will transfer their fear to others which makes others fear too, which should be changed.

During takeoff I was not frightened, though it was my first time, I never had that fear, instead my friend who was very strong and always boasted that fear never came near him, got frightened at the time of takeoff. People who talk a lot are very much frightened to face problems or any issues, they know only to chit chat, like that my friend kept on chatting, till we reached our destination he never stopped talking. Oh my I couldn't sleep, frankly I never enjoyed my flight, rather I kept on listening to useless stories. Finally we reached our destination, though he talked and boasted he helped me a lot in handling my luggage and in the airport as well for the rest of the procedures, since I was new to the place this guy had some idea about an airport, so it was easy for me, he made it easy. As soon as I reached there I called my parents to say that I was safe and secure, the employer had sent someone in the airport with a vehicle to pick us up, so we got inside the vehicle and travelled to our apartment. The country has its own beauty, it was not like India, the whole country seemed to be busy all the time and very crowded, it is totally a metro life with big apartments and flats. We reached our company owned flat, I and three other colleagues from Kerala were allocated a two bedroom flat, which was on the seventh floor, the accommodation was on a sharing basis, two per one bedroom. I was stunned looking at the facilities they provided for the employees, it was a five star category accommodation, it was a two bedroom apartment with a hall and a kitchen with three attached bathrooms, they had everything like sofa, refrigerators, washing machine, air conditioned room, gas connections, microwave oven, toasting machine and so many things. My friends were very happy seeing all these facilities which the company provided and they were stunned. I was stunned looking at that, but after a while when I thought about work I felt homesick, but no turning back. The career started with a sad note, it was not my cup of tea.

break the suspense of my wife's love story, her parents accepted her love, her father had to return from abroad in order to take a decision, and finally her elder sisters marriage, now the suspense was whether the boy's parents accepted his love or not, before that she fell in love with him so deep within. Their journey of love continued for one year, and in this one year the boy kept on convincing the girl that his parents would accept their relationship. His family is very traditional, this guy was very much frightened of his parents, at the same time he never did anything without the knowledge of his parents, she always had the fear whether this relationship would continue or not, but somewhere in her heart she had confidence. Her father came and after some days he called up this guy to talk about marriage, the father liked him because he was so innocent, he spoke very nicely, but one thing father said was he was not financially sound, but he liked his daughter very much, whatever was her wish it was her father's wish too. The boy listened to all this, and said "Let me discuss with my parents and I will tell you an answer." Meanwhile this girl was so happy and was excited, and at that time she was very serious about her career. At that time the girl's parents were very seriously looking for an alliance for their elder daughter and the youngest one was dreaming about her future with her life partner. Even in that her elder sister never liked the boy she chose, she was not satisfied with her selection but she liked him so she never bothered about her sister. Whenever you expect happiness in life it always gives you sadness, at the same time if you are sad unexpectedly, life gives you happiness. She too had such a moment in life when her boyfriend suddenly broke up with her without telling her. Love is a journey you don't know, when accident happens at the time of the journey, the same with love, an accident happens, you get hurt, but should have the courage to bear the pain, else you end up in the middle of the journey losing yourself. Say if you are planning to do a long journey on your vacation, the key factor is your state of mind and happiness, if you don't have either of these factors it is worthless continuing the journey, the same applies in love, happiness and your state of mind is the key to love. You can imagine what happens when a boy suddenly breaks up and disappears all of a sudden, you can imagine the emotions from a girl's point, put yourself in her shoes, a person who knows what true love is can understand her emotions. Some can tell the boy cheated on her, his parents never agreed, time passes, in love one can keep on giving excuses, but what is real apart from excuses is the situation, the situation is strictly for people who follow true love, people who just see love in other aspects it's not situation, it's playful. Situations here are the factor for her emotional tragedy, so you may ask what that situation is.

What is situation? Is it something we create, or is it something which happens unexpectedly? I always had confusion about this all my life, what makes a situation worse, happy, sad and angry. It's just the circumstances in which one finds oneself. We act in life according to circumstances, the situation has been created and it depends on how an individual overcomes that situation.

Getting into college life, a life which decides your future, if you ask somcone how were your college days, no one will ever say that they never enjoyed that life, they will always say that they miss that life, because they say they were very happy only during that time of their school and college life. I have seen friends who chose their course thinking about their future benefits, not because they like it, so nowadays they choose a course and when it comes to a career they are into a different stream, it's because of unemployment, when the population increases obviously unemployment increases. As I said, I took a subject which was easy for me to study, so I never had any difficulty, when it came to my career it was entirely different, it's not because I never wanted to follow a career that I studied, but I was not interested, everyone in my family asked me, "Why did you take up a course if you couldn't continue the same for your career?" Yes I agree the fact. But my interests and passion differed. I have seen friends as soon they complete twelfth grade they start dreaming about their college life, and they have a total different concept about college, most of them think that college is a place you can show your courage and your freedom, nowadays everyone likes to stay away from the house and do their studies abroad, it's not because they don't have any other options, it's because they need freedom to enjoy their life, so the concept about a college changes when people start to think about fun. People who take studies very seriously, college is their platform and people think college is the place to have fun, the track changes, people who enjoy both fun and studies, then that's their station to wait for the arrival of future and continue the journey to their mission. Compared to school life, college life is where you get absolute freedom, when I was studying, ragging in college was in its peak, though they made ragging an offence you could find some incidents happening in some college, I too have faced ragging, to be frank I was very frightened when my friends discussed about some incidents that happened in other colleges, that was the first time I started to realize what college actually means, I took a decision to stay away from home and study because I had no other choice, the course which I took was not available in our place, and there were not many colleges where I stayed. All these things made me choose a college which is far from my place, after my college admission my concept regarding college changed because of my friend, so I planned to face the college life with some courage. I never stayed in the college hostel, instead I stayed with one my cousin brother and with two other friends, taking an individual house.

College life will teach equal good and bad, more friends, it's how you show dedication to studies, I started my journey in college, as I expected the course was not that difficult, they had more practicals than theory classes. I never had an interest in the course I took, but my mind was fixed to that course because it was easy. When you take college life, this is the place you will start to realize your self esteem, if you take schools whether it be dress, friends, teachers and other activities they follow a rule, but college is of no rules whether it be dress, friends, teachers and whatever they have their own style. You know what college is all about, so I don't have to explain about it in detail; me and my roommates were in the same class so we used to go together to the class everyday, since that's our first year we were frightened of ragging. For the first few weeks college students were very silent, at that it was an offence if they found students ragging first year, so for a few days our professors and teaches secured us in college, after few weeks students started ragging. I started to hate college life, how can students behave so violently? What shocked me is even girls were included in these kinds of activities. Some took it sportive, but I was not able to be so, what they do is not right, my first year in college I faced a lot of difficulties, we entered into second year, now my friends started to plan the same concept for the upcoming first year students, which I said was wrong, but there was no respect. It does not mean that we should follow the same custom that our seniors were following, instead they committed the same mistake. So even in my college days I was left alone, I don't usually stick with activities which I feel are not right, from the second year my friends started to avoid me for so many reasons, at times I felt very lonely even though I stayed with them. My friends started to fight with me for no reason, in the middle of the second year a new roommate joined our room, he had a soft corner with me. You know the main problem with friends if they have a friend who is different from others, in his thoughts or he is trying to be good and at the same time making them also good, then that guy is left alone. I have come across so many incidents like that in my life, good will not reach you quickly, it takes its time. How long can you stay alone in the room when others are having fun, so as days passed I tried to change my character, I started to bring out an evil nature, you cannot judge a human when he becomes evil or when he becomes good, but the living environment decides?

Do you remember that I was talking about a crush which I had when I was in ninth grade and never expressed? A day came in my life to express my emotion towards her; I will never call this love, I don't want to use the word called love for attraction like others do. She was in eleventh grade, I had spoke to her twice, once when I became popular with the nickname and secondly at the time of school sports, but I didn't know her name, I have never admired her, or been friendly with her but I was attracted to her; one day during children's day festival she happened to speak with me once more for help from me with her friend, that was the first time I actually looked at her face so close, usually boys get attracted to girls for their beauty or their character, but the majority is their beauty, even when you take marriage the boy and the girl express their likings, looking at each other's physical appearance, which I call attraction, in love attraction comes in the form of beauty. No one will look in for character, this is quite natural, and attraction comes first, and then comes the character. Most love stories fail for this reason because there is no understanding. I too followed the attraction formula, I was attracted to her smile, she had a cute smile which reminded me of my mid school girl, maybe that might be a reason I liked her, so she asked me to do a favor, I said, "It's my pleasure," in a sweet voice, she asked me to buy some eatables from outside the school, since they were in hostel they were not allowed to go out of the school or buy eatables from outside, when she said this I asked her, "If teachers or your hostel warden finds this I will get into trouble." In return, she said, "If you can help, you help, I will ask this favor from someone else who is capable," which my ego never let me, so I agreed to do the favor. I wondered from where I got the courage to do all this, the next day I bought all the eatables which she mentioned in the list she gave me, I could give this to her only during break time, during break time I went to see her in her class and saw her sitting with a boy, and I handed over the eatables which she asked me to buy, and asked the boy frankly, "Are you her boyfriend?" Those days, when we said boyfriend it meant lover, that age do not have the maturity to think whether it is a friend or brother whatever, because the circle we are in makes us think like that. So what I asked insulted the boy and he started to shout at me saying mind your own business, and the conversation became lengthy, at the same time the girl was having nice fun seeing this, which made me think she never even said thanks for the help I gave, instead making fun of me. It's my mistake, I don't know what made me ask the boy that question, the school bell rang and silently I went back to my class without even saying sorry for my mistake, at that time I never knew what else to do. This incident turned out to be an issue with eleventh grade students and ninth grade students, I had no other choice to admit my mistake in front of others, that was my first bad experience that happened in my school, after that I never looked at her, I just forgot everything and started to concentrate on my studies.

After buying eatables for those girls, everyone else came and asked me to do the same favor, because that girl mentioned my name in the hostel, knowing that everyone started to ask me to buy eatables, I had no choice to say no to them. I already did a favor and that too to a girl, if I said no to others, then they would say that he helps only girls, so I thought that should not happen, buying eatables became a hobby in school, even kids started to utilize me for this. After this incident my friends advised me a lot for which I never bothered because they never advised properly, instead they said, "If you do something without asking us, then you will face these kind of consequences," so I said "it's my personal right to do what I feel like doing, I am the one who is facing the consequences, if there is an issue I don't come asking help from you, if there is a situation like that then you can advise," which they never liked. They thought that I was acting to be big, after I became popular in school, yes even at times I had realized that I was trying to act big, this was my ego. I observed a change in me after I became popular in school which led to so many issues, but I always I faced it individually, the whole class started to hate me even when I was silent, and even now, when I am not silent. Change yourself not your character, try to be and don't try to become.

Friends started to make fun of me saying that I am a loser, but one thing they noticed that I had the courage to speak to anyone without fear, so friends came to me asking for a favor, before knowing what that favor is let's get back to an incident which happened in my life unexpectedly, which made rethink about love once again.

I thought the attraction towards a girl during mid school had come to an end when I came from that school, I totally forgot her, though I remembered her at times I never took it that seriously, when I was in ninth grade I happened to visit my old school for a function since one of my teachers who stayed near my house compelled me to attend the function. I went for that function, it was some religious function they conducted in the school church. When I entered the old school my thoughts provoked me, I started to visualize memories about that school, the feeling was strange, this happens to everyone who has sweet memories in school and college, some memories cannot be forgotten the reason is those memories have not been fulfilled, some memories haunt you for a lifetime. When I was working in

Hyderabad, I had a friend who was my roommate, we both worked in different companies, he was from Bangalore, but he had a special talent which I liked. He was a multi-lingual person, he spoke almost five languages and he was so fluent in all five languages, he knew Hindi, Tamil, English, Kannada (native language of Bangalore) and Telugu and he was learning French, Sanskrit, Arabic and Urdu. He loved travelling, he had visited almost all the places in India as well as abroad. I have never seen him sad, he was so funny and always had a smile on his face, he had a girlfriend who lived in Bangalore and they were in love with each other for more than eight years, and both of their parents had accepted their relationship and they were about to get engaged. Before the engagement he was sent to New Delhi for a project by his employer. The project was for two weeks, and after two weeks he came to the room, but I noticed a change in him when he came. He was totally different, he seemed to be lost, he was a person who seemed to be happy and smiling, so all of a sudden he became so silent missing his happiness. I never asked him anything, I thought it's not fair to interfere; one day his girlfriend called me telling me that his phone was switched off and this guy had never spoken to her after he came from Delhi. I asked her, "How come you got my number?" and she answered, "My friend gave your number in case of emergency."

This guy had a habit of writing everything in his diary; after his girlfriend told me to inform him that she was expecting his call to know what his problem was, I said, "I will inform my friend that you called me." I had so many questions, I even thought to peek in his diary, but instincts never allowed me to do that so I waited for this guy to come from the office. That night he was drunk, he drinks very occasionally, but that night he seemed to be drunk on purpose, so I thought it wasn't fair to ask him when he was in that stage, so that night I kept my mouth shut. The next day I made a strong tea and I gave it to him, and he too took it. Very casually, I asked about his trip to Delhi, I had a fear to ask him about his problem. I didn't know how he would react if I asked him, but my mind was tempting me to ask him. I told him that his girlfriend called, and that she was expecting his call, he answered in a very low tone, OK, and he said, "I have to go to the office a little early today," so I never asked him anything, when leaving for the office he called me and said, "I will come early in the evening, and let's go for a walk. I have something important to tell you," and he left for the office. I too agreed to come early in the evening, I was very clear that he was going to tell me the reason for his change.

Later that evening, I reached the flat a little early and I saw my friend sitting and having a conversation over the phone. I just saw him and nodded my head. I understood that he was talking to his parents because he kept on saying Dad frequently, but that conversation seemed to be very serious so I just went to my room and closed my eyes because I was so tired. With that tiredness, I slept well, when I woke up it was already nine in the evening so I went to the hall looking for him, he was still holding the phone and having a serious conversation, but this time he was speaking with his girlfriend, usually when speaking to girls, boys sound different. I don't have to explain, everyone knows that. After some time he called me and said sorry. I said, "No problem," and he continued telling me what happened in the two weeks when he was in Delhi. When he went for the project he was not alone, he had two other friends with him for the same project, from accommodation till food everything was taken care of by the company, he was a team manager in that company so he had some concession, the project and the work was going fine for two weeks, the project was successful so to celebrate it the company had a party organized, this party was about to commence the day before my friend was returning to Hyderabad, when you say metro parties you can imagine how that party is, everything was going fine until he got drunk. He started to consume alcohol till he lost his state of mind and he was totally out, the next day morning when he woke up he saw a girl sleeping next to him, and it was a hotel, he was not able to remember anything which happened last night so he was so confused, the girl woke up and saw her mobile and thought she was already late, and she got ready in a hurry, he tried to ask her what really happened last night, but in return she answered, "Don't act as if you don't know anything." My friend was telling the truth, but she was not able to believe this and in a hurry she left the hotel, now this guy was in a dilemma, what happened? He couldn't remember, that was his problem. After some time his friends came to the room and asked him how last night was. He tried to ask them what really happened, and they said, "You picked her up from the party and you brought her here, that's what we know apart from that I don't know anything." Friends said, "If you can't remember anything that means you have been drugged." He was totally drowned. With that confusion he had to fly back to Hyderabad, his mind was haunting, he couldn't stop from his memories, imagine a guy who lives in sweet memories and all of a sudden something bitter happens, he knows he did commit a mistake and now he is trying to overcome it, this made him upset, caused him to lose his happiness, and created all sort of disturbances in his life. This continued for almost two weeks after he came back, so finally he told his parents what happened, what can parents do about this at this time? He is soon going to get engaged with a girl he has loved for more than eight years. How can he ditch all these things that were troubling him? His parents suggested that he meet that girl once again, he had no contact number, he didn't know where she worked he didn't know where she lived and knew nothing about her whereabouts. So he finally decided to be honest with his girlfriend, so he told her the truth. You know how girls react if they come to know the hidden truth, yes you are very correct, none of the girls respect their honesty so she broke up. We can't blame the girl either, she thought about her safety and security in her life, so immediately she left the guy, there was no second chance, the boy tried to be honest because he thought nothing should be a secret in relationship, which shows how much he loved that girl. Life had some weird twist, after that he lived with his memories, till I was working in Hyderabad he was not married, after that I never had any contact with him, either. It's good to remember your past memories, but never live with it.

So once again I had a chance to visit my old school because of my teacher, so when I looked at my old classrooms, school grounds, class benches this girl was coming to my mind, for a few seconds I thought if I had a chance to see her once again that would be great, and all of a sudden someone from behind called my name, and when I turned back I could see her standing in front of me, the girl who I admired, who I was attracted to for the first time, there standing right in front of me. I thought 'How come she is here, is it my dream?' and after some time I remembered her saying that she would continue in the same school since it was a girls' higher secondary school. I was seeing her after four years, she spoke to me, well obviously now she was not the same fifth standard girl, when I saw her I never felt anything, no sweet imaginations or dreams. She asked me so many questions, I had never seen her like this talking to me but there was a change in her. So I asked her, "How is your boyfriend?" She smiled and said, "That guy forgot me as soon as he left the school." She asked me, "Do you at least remember me, now my imaginations began in different angles, why was she asking me this at this moment? With confusion I said to her, "No time to remember anything, was so busy." Again with a smile, she asked, "Are you so very busy in studies?" I said "Yes, I am busy studying," and I was laughing inside. I asked her, "How come you recognized me after so many years?" She said she never forgot. I was not able to speak anything more, now my heart started to beat heavily, I can hear those beats very clearly, it was like I was about to die, she invited me to her house when I was free to come and visit her grandmother and her parents. I said if possible I would come, and I said "Teacher is waiting for me, so I have to take leave from here." She gave me a smile and she went with her friends, her friends were looking at me very strangely because they could not believe this girl was talking to me, because all the time she had avoided me. In four years she has grown fat, and I was so lean, that's the only difference I could feel. At the same time I think my heart once again started to wake up to dive into the ocean of love. Love is an ocean, it never drains; you can swim in that ocean a number of times, but remember that you don't get drained with it. My heart once again started to strike the name of love, once again when I saw her. After the function I left the school, before leaving I searched for her thinking to see her once again, standing in front of the church hearing the school bell ring, she came out of her class. I was about to leave but she came with her friends and introduced me to others as well. I noticed that she was feeling shy, a girl with shyness in her face made me admire her beauty, once again with so much excitement, I felt like I was in the ocean feeling the chillness of the water and kept on swimming with a state of unconscious mind. Suddenly I came back to reality when she said "Let's walk together." There are no words to express my happiness, I felt like I was a blessed soul, she kept on talking and kept on admiring, she stopped talking at a spot where we had to leave in two different ways, so she said bye with a smile. I too gave a smile and said bye. I never expected that I would meet this girl today, but it just happened in a few seconds when I thought of her. So the day went well and good, don't conclude that I was in love, I myself don't know that.

People have their magic moments in life; there is a phrase in the Bible "Unless you see signs and wonders you will not believe." Finishing my college, I was into a different career, I studied something and I ended up choosing a different career. I had been to different companies, gained experience in the service industry. I started my career without any interest, but I don't know somehow I was interested in service jobs. I started liking it as days continued, when I was working in Chennai, at that time I accidently happened to speak with a girl through one of my far distant relatives, since they needed a small favor from my end. I had never seen her, but I knew for sure that she was somehow related, so I happened to call her, but that conversation started to build friendship as days moved on, whenever a relationship starts and if someone comes to know that then the blame is on the boy, girls are always left free from blame. When I initially called her, she knew that it was a new number and she was about to speak with a stranger she did not know. The girl had already been informed by my relatives that I would call her at some point of time, but she did not know when that would happen. If I am not wrong I called her in the evening time, as soon as she answered the call she said "Hi sweetheart," I was shocked, maybe she was expecting a call from someone .I was thinking maybe I called her and disturbed her at the wrong time, so I dropped the call and I sent her a message stating sorry, and I kept quiet. After few seconds I got a buzz on my mobile and the message was "Don't play with me. I know you are so and so, and there was some name given who I don't even know, so I thought it better to reveal my identity, if not that would be a problem." So I called her once again and I told her who I was, and the purpose of my call. She was totally taken aback for a moment and then she apologized for a moment for what happened. I too never asked anything because I was not interested in knowing her personal details. After a few days she called me once again, just for a casual chat, and she kept on talking about her personal life and about her friends and so on, then buzzing became very frequent. Conversations were regular, during office hours, holidays, weekends, weekdays but we never met. I didn't even know what she looked like. Our friendship continued for just a few months, and then we had some issues personally and we stopped chatting for a while, but that girl kept on calling me, let me not get into that story in deep because the story is not related to the magic moment in my life. It was just a beginning to a new life, in the name of love some stupid things happened, but till the end I never met her, but the girl made me realize the real meaning of love. During that time I was confused with love, my mind was totally disturbed so I just shifted from Chennai to Hyderabad to a different company. One year I was totally invisible, I never had any contacts with anyone for that fact, no emails, no mobile, I was totally left all alone, on the other end my parents were worried, in this one year I was trying to overcome my mind's views on love, as everyone says there is a time for everyone in life, realizing the moment in life.

One year totally undisturbed in another company, I did part time jobs in the Telugu media industry for a few months, in this one year I realized a lot of things about life. Life taught me a lot of good stuff, I realized about love, parents, friends and most importantly God. All those years I never believed in God, but someone unknown to me and to this world made me realize what is life and love. An incident which happened when I was in Hyderabad made me realize that God exists. Magic moments happen in everyone's life, but from that very moment you are trying to implement those moments in life. I can hear your mind's voice, that you are totally confused else you are very eager to know the magic which made him realize God. Before that magic incident, I had a dream where my grandfather came in my dream and said I wanted to see you where you are, which made me think of my family after one year, within that year there were a lot of changes in my family, after one year I called my parents and they were so happy to hear my voice and they were very eager to see me, obviously after one year you are contacting your parents, till then they were very much frightened for their son who never contacted them for so long.

As soon as I called them, the very first thing I asked them was about my grandfather and the news which I heard from them was that he had passed away, which made me upset. So I agreed to reach home in a few weeks, after I heard that news I was not able to concentrate on my work or anything, then I checked my emails, my brother had tried to contact me through emails and he had shared the news of my grandfather's death in email. But it was my mistake that

I never looked into emails, I couldn't concentrate on work after I came to know my grandfathers death. So I finally planned to leave that job and go back to my house and see my parents. Before leaving for home I happened to meet a stranger who made me realize who God is. Now who is this stranger, what did he speak, what really happened after that, what made him realize that there is a God? I know these questions will arise in your mind which should be answered; of course your questions will be answered.

After one year I went back to my house and my parents felt so happy when they saw me, they are seeing me after one year, so you can imagine how their expressions were. They saw me and felt a change in me which they could not believe; all those years I was not a good son, friend, neighbor, employee or a good brother. Now I had totally changed, within a few days they understood my maturity level in things which I did, before that I was playful with my life. I began a new life after that magic happened in my life, everything in life was going smooth until then, but somewhere I missed something in my life. Life is not an easy journey, through that journey we tend to forget things which have to be followed in life, what are those things? Let's dive into that journey.

Let's continue with my high school journey, I realized my crush with a senior girl would never be possible so I just stopped admiring her, instead I concentrated on my studies. My friends came to me asking for a favor, there was a friend in our group who was behind a girl for two years, she was in seventh grade when was in ninth, she was our junior, so this guy asked me to go and propose on behalf of him; when I thought about the incident which happened for me I was frightened once again, I couldn't apologize in front of others, so I told him "I am not coming to play that game and I am not interested in helping a friend for this, if you don't have the courage to propose then don't love," and I started to avoid him. None of my friends spoke to me just because I said I couldn't help him. I too never bothered, the whole year got completed and we were entering into tenth grade. My friends remained the same even in tenth grade, they never allowed me to join their group. One day during class hours the same guy came to me asking for the same help, but this time I agreed to help him with one condition, "I will not speak to her, rather you write a letter. I will just give her that letter and the rest you take care of." He too agreed and wrote a letter for her.

She was in eight, I could give the letter only during break time. I took the letter and went to her class, my friends helped me to spot the girl and I went forward with the letter. I called her by her name and as soon as she turned back, I got stunned, and it was like electricity passing over my body, she was so beautiful, she had blue eyes, very fair, brownish short hair, a cute smile, but not Indian– she was a Canadian girl. For a few seconds I travelled to a different world, but when I thought my friend had the crush I just stopped dreaming and I gave her the letter and I just returned back without telling her anything. My friends were very eagerly waiting outside to know the answer, but she just took the letter and did not say anything, so I told my friends that my work was over, and the rest is in their hands, and I never interfered.

Days moved on, my friend was still waiting for an answer from that girl, but there was no response, friends kept on compelling me to speak with her once again, but I said no. After a few days this girl came to my class, I thought she was going to meet my friend but instead she came near me, the rest of the class was watching this show and I was frightened, she came near me and she kept on shouting at me and the whole class was listening to the conversation and finally she gave me a slap and threw the letter in my face and she left. I knew she was angry, but one thing I never understood was why did she show her anger to me instead of showing it to my friend? The whole class looked at me and was laughing, already they knew that I had a crush with a girl so everyone thought when that never happened he tried with some other girl which created a bad impression on me, but I never minded because I knew I hadn't done anything wrong, but I had some confusion about why she reacted to me so I took the letter and started reading it. The letter had no name, it was just a letter expressing one's emotions with a proposal. Obviously the girl thought I proposed to her, it was my mistake that I believed my friends so I trusted them, my friend came to me and apologized for his mistake, I never reacted to anyone. See what popularity had for me? I was becoming more popular with unexpected incidents, because of me and my friends, I never blamed anyone, instead, I took the blame myself. It's not because I wanted to purposely take the blame myself, I thought it was a not a good idea to justify what happened. After that the impression totally changed and everyone started avoiding me. At some point of life you will have to face some or the other difficulties, if you take it seriously then it will become an issue, I was not worried about anyone, instead I just moved on with life as it led.

Trust, how many of us truly believe in it? You cannot trust anyone in this world if you don't trust yourself, I would say parents are the best examples for trust, their trust is unbreakable. I have personally experienced in my life, it is we as kids that break their trust, but still they will trust you. I would like to share a love story which happened to a friend of mine, this guy is a passionate guy, his passion, the Internet. You will not see him without a laptop, he is always active in all social networking sites, and he surfs a lot. The Internet is his friend; he sleeps and works with it, so you can imagine how many friends he would have for a guy who is online twenty four seven. So he had so many girlfriends and boyfriends, when I say girlfriends he had so many end numbers, he is very rich, he does not care about the money that he spends, he spends a lot. He used the word love with all girls he spoke to, as soon as the girl is friendly he proposes to the girl and somehow he convinces the girl to fall for him. What surprised me is that all these girls who fell for him because they trusted him, I have advised him so many times not to cheat girls in the name of trust, but he said it's his personal life, don't interfere, so I never interfered. I don't know how boys can convince girls in such a way, never spoil trust in the name of love, love is pure, there are so many boys and girls out there spoiling trust in the name of love, not only love, friendship and marriage, all these are trust based, try to hold that trust. Now it is a situation in this world that no one can trust each other because the society is like that, they don't know the real meaning of trust. I can't change the world but it's a small message from my side, "Love is trust based, don't spoil that." It's up to you whether to take this note or not.

My abroad career life started after so many complications and troubles with less interest in the job, six months probation and two years contract, no option to quit in the middle, three months of job training, once the training is successful then you go live. Once again, I happened to visit different cultured people from different countries after my high school; training sessions were like a honeymoon period, nothing much. I started to like the training sessions, it was so much fun, it was a safety critical job, though it was a service industry which was my stream. This was the first time I was into a safety based service job. At some point I fell in love with the job, I usually don't love my job but I will never fail to do the given job, after training I went live with the work, meeting people from different countries, knowing their culture, travelled to different places, visited so many places, in one year I became very fluent in the job which I did, though I had some issues with my friends that never disturbed me. I had a colleague who stayed with me who was full of jealousy. I never bothered about anything, I just worked and I was so happy. I was never happy with the other jobs which I did previously with other employers, it was the first time ever I stayed in a company for one year, once you know you are about to get settled, the very next thing which comes to mind is marriage, a life partner, someone to love you for the rest of your life. So I decided to get married and shared my opinion with my parents, and they too agreed, and they started to look in for brides.

I don't believe in this so called astrology, but my father was a true believer, when they were looking for a bride I strictly informed my parents to tell the girl's family that they shouldn't demand anything, it is just the marriage. I think you would have understood in simple, I hate dowry, but you know society and relatives they are always very eager in finding out how much the girl's family is ready to give. If you take relatives and friends they are always behind one's assets, they don't motivate one's growth, instead they like to interfere in one's problems.

There is a tradition that Hindus follow, when it comes to marriage they look in for caste, religion, background, society, relatives, friends, career, and status and then finally marriage comes. Mine was not that qualitative, though the girls followed this tradition, I never looked for all these, all I looked for is love. I would say from the girl's end this marriage was an accident, but from my side it was dedication towards love. I never had any difficult in finding a bride, nowadays you have so many websites where you can register your name and they select a girl according to matchings done by given information in the website by both bride and the groom. So I just registered my name in it, after registering I never had any response for a few days, I never searched much for matching brides diving in that website, I had confidence one day someone would come in search of me. After a few days I received an email from the bride's end with their phone number, stating that if interested just get back to the number. As soon as I saw that email I never had any second thought, I decided that she was going to be my girl. I don't know what made me think so, but that was my final decision. Remember that I hadn't spoke with the parents nor had I met her, but my mind was fixed with the decision to marry her. You may wonder how it can be possible, it is the real fact.

Rewinding back to the life which my wife had before marriage, after her father had a conversation with the boy, the boy told her father that his parents were not accepting the marriage, "And your daughter is the one who compelled me to love her," which left her father doubtful. He thought that the boy was not serious; the boy left her a goodbye note to the relationship and travelled far. Maybe the boy had issues in convincing his parents, but here the girl lost her trust, from the beginning she had no confidence in love, as expected their relationship had not worked out. So the father advised his daughter and explained what the boy told him, which she never believed, instead she never believed her father, now everyone started to blame her that the mistake was hers, but she never bothered about all those blaming something made her to believe that her boyfriend is innocent. After he left her, she became very upset, she was not able to work or concentrate, which made her lose happiness. By seeing this, her family members also lost their happiness, this is what I say about creating situations, we create problems in life unnecessarily instead of accepting life as it goes, we are fighting for life, which is stupid. So the girl for several days punished herself in different ways, sitting all alone, not conversing with others, not being active and so many things. Do you think these are the remedies in life? But what to do, some characters are like this, we cannot change them until they change themselves.

She tried to contact him, but the guy totally disappeared, but I would blame him, instead of running, if he would have convinced her there would not be any problems, but he never did that. Instead of speaking with the girl who was involved, he spoke with her sister and father about his problems, not only that he told her sister that she was blackmailing him to love her, but when you read her story it is not like that, but the boy reacted differently, he complained about her character and so on, which he never said to the girl he loved. When her sister and father complained about the boy's character she could not believe it, she believed a boy who she knew only for one year, which left her family members disappointed. I have heard people telling me love is dangerous, why is it dangerous? It is dangerous because we feel so apart from that it is not dangerous. So she herself started to imagine things about her future, she even thought there was no use living this life without him. I don't know why people react stupidly, when in love they forget parents, they just remember their love is the one and only important factor, and the rest becomes invisible which I feel is not healthy.

I had a friend who had the same situation, in the name of love there are people who attempt to spoil their life, attempting suicide, spoiling others' happiness. In the name of love there are a few other people who try to exploit girls, and even girls try to exploit boys and vice versa, they don't really care about their life or hurting others, generations have been changed, love became a hobby, the days are gone where love is treated as a soulful experience or a divine essence in life. You are surrounded with love in your life, parents' love, friends' love, world's love, neighbors' love, brother and sister's love, teachers love and so on, your life is full of love. At a certain age you choose a girl to love, if it succeeds well and good else you forget all others' love in the name of love, people tend to forget what is real love if love never succeeds in life, and that too for a boy or a girl.

Let's continue with my friend's love which my friend feels is tragic in his life. Two years behind a girl, three years with a girl as a friend, one year waiting for an answer from the girl after expressing his love, two years with a girl after she accepted his love, after which the journey of love stopped and now it's been three years there is no love, and this guy was addicted to alcohol. In the name of love he spoiled himself and his happiness which led his family members to a great disappointment, there were reasons and issues which I think are totally garbage, there was no love when he explained it to me, he said he was in love with that girl for the past eight years and he is the only reason for the girl to leave him and why do you make your life a tragic moment. I don't want to explain his love story in detail because I feel it's a total waste of time because their love lacked logic, but I just wanted to convey that we spoil our own life in the name of love which should be avoided, instead realize there is life.

My wife for few months was upset in the name of love, her thought was what her friends and relatives thought about her, which made her more frightened as months and days moved on. Her elder sister's marriage was nearing, which made her think that she should do something for her elder sister's marriage financially since they were not that financially energetic. So she started to work for the family to keep her engaged and forget the past memories. Though she started a new life somewhere at the corner she looked in for the boy who disappeared, but she took her work seriously, seeing this her parents felt happy and everything was going on fine.

I became an average student in studies when I reached tenth grade, due to lack of concentration, everyone will be frightened of tenth board examination but I was not worried. I never took studies that seriously, I always showed last minute seriousness in studies. I used to sit alone in class when others did group studies, once when I was a bright student I never used to join any group, so this avoiding never disturbed me in any way. There were reasons for them to avoid me, I too know and the readers you to know it, but reality is something else. After a few incidents in school I became silent once again in my life, I realized how popularity creates a bad impression if you don't handle it well, it's easy to earn a bad name, but to erase that bad name is not that easy. I realized this very lately, my ego led me to troubles and complications when I was in tenth grade, but it never stopped permanently, it was just a temporary realization. When you feel lonely you tend to imagine all these things, but when fame strikes once again you are back with the same ego which happened to me once again. Tenth board examinations were finished, I still don't know how I managed to complete my tenth, the way I prepared for the board exams I myself thought I would not move to eleventh grade. At the time of examination, whenever I took the book I fell asleep, if tomorrow was my exam I would start to prepare for that exam only that morning before the exam. I have entered the exam hall at times not knowing what exam was going to commence, that's how my seriousness was during board exams. But the question paper was so easy it was not that difficult. I did my examinations with the knowledge which I had, at times I used to listen in class which helped me a lot at the time of my exams. When the result came I scored good marks, which made my parents happy, even they thought that I would not pass, but they never expected that I would pass so that's how I managed to pass my tenth board examinations. Study hard, you will get the result, I don't believe in that fact, instead listen to class and try to grab and understand what they are teaching, you don't have to study, you can just go through the text book once without any tension or pressure, you can score good marks. If you do something keeping in mind that you will not succeed then the outcome will be the same, at the same time if you do something without any expectation the outcome will be unexpected. Never pressure yourself in doing things, and don't do things in a confused state of mind always try and do things very happily.

When I entered into eleventh grade I became senior and my senior crush had already completed her twelfth and left the school, so I never had to bow my head when I crossed twelfth grade in school. Everything else remained the same, friends, teachers and the girl who slapped me. Now my classmates forgot everything happened at the time of tenth grade, we became friends once again, no grudge or revenge, it was a new beginning as seniors. The school had a system, those who performed well in their academics and other competitions in school would review students' attendance and their performance and they picked each one from a different class to be the prefect, school captain, house captain, vice captain, and rank holders. When I say house captain, here the school had four different houses and every year they picked a house and they awarded the best house of the year based on reviews and performance. So every year in the beginning they selected students, our class students were expecting the same, and students were excited as to who would become the class leader and other title holders for the year. After a long time I got a second rank badge, once again when I was in eleventh, one day our class teacher called for a students' meeting, so I participated, I knew they were discussing to decide the title holders for the year. After that meeting they said that they were about to give me a prefect and house vice captain position based on my performance in school, I was happy hearing that, at the same time something stopped me from getting those titles, so I said I was not interested, so they never compelled me after that. After that meeting, when I went back to the class everyone started to ask me what happened in that meeting. I explained to them about what happened in there, everyone started laughing at me hearing that, they never believed that I was chosen for that, no one even had a hope. I was upset, I had no idea what made them not believe me, but they never believed me. So I personally went to the staff room where my class teacher was sitting and I went and told her the reality of what happened, and I strictly told her not to mention that I was chosen for these titles, let it be a joke and she too agreed. My mind was running over thoughts to find a reason why they never believed me, was it because I was not that smart, or was it because I never participated in any competitions, or was it because I was not eligible, there were so many questions. After this there was an election conducted in our class to select a class leader. I knew for sure no one would vote for me, as expected I never became the class leader. There will be a twist in everyone's life which happens without your knowledge, in simple terms "expect the unexpected." Let's see what that unexpected twist was.

There were two twists in my life which I never expected when I was in eleventh grade, friends joined me and once again asked me for a favor, the same guy who asked me to give the letter to the girl, now she is in ninth grade and this guy was still behind her. But this time the favor was in the form of sympathy, as soon as I heard what he said, I said no on the spot. You want know what he said? This is what he said, he wanted to create a drama where I would play the role of villain and he would be the hero who would create sympathy and justify his mistake in the name of love. Obviously, if he does that now after a long time it would be good, but it's too late to justify his mistake, it would be like I was giving him a chance to create a sympathy love out of it, but I asked him to admit his mistake in front of the class which he denied so I said I would not agree to his favor to play heroism. But unfortunately without my permission he tried to make me villain, explaining this to the girl that he was the one who wrote the letter and never had the courage to express it to her, so he utilized his friend to know what would be the outcome of the letter. He did this keeping in mind that he could capture her love by creating sympathy, which was absolute stupid, at that time even I didn't know the consequences, and my friend too never thought what would happen next.

After that incident, the next day my class boarding girls were looking at me and were smiling at me which was good to see. I had never seen them giving me such respect, everyone called me to tell me what happened, why there was a sudden change in them, at that time I came to know that this girl shared the truth with my class girls, which made them think that I did something great, which my friend never thought such a twist from the incident, according to him what he did was correct, if I had agreed to that favor it would be like I was trying to create some drama to justify my mistake, and I didn't know what made him do so, but his thought was wrong, which my friend never liked and now everyone started to dislike him except his friends. It was like Facebook, if you like something you have an option to like it else an option to dislike, it was something similar to that. The class girls changed their attitude all of a sudden. Now once again I became the known figure in school doing something great, but I never felt that I did something great. I had no other choice, the same class who had a bad impression suddenly changed but I went to my friend and I asked him, "Did I ask you to do this?" And I said, "Not to worry, I will be with you and I will help you in your love, and I made him smile at me. If someone does something wrong you shouldn't do the same to him, when you get a chance rather try to be different, which is what I did. This twist never includes two twists which happened in my life. I haven't started to talk about it.

God, who is he, is he your love, is he your father or mother, is he your brother or sister, is he your friend, is he your lifeguard who saves you in critical situations, is he your master, is he within you, is he outside this world, is he in heaven, is he your role model, is he your superhero, is he unknown what is he? I had all these questions within when

I never believed that God exists in this world. If I am not wrong I never even bothered to know about what is God, I have always thought is it a subject to get involved, I had this mind for almost thirty years in my life, I often used to visit temples just to observe the beauty of silence not to praise or demand, even now I will tell the same that temples, churches and mosques are places to observe the beauty of silence they're not places to demand happiness, money, children or whatever assets in life. I don't believe God gives you what you demand, that it's our personal belief, I am not blaming any individual's belief here and I don't mean that God does not exist; it's each individual's belief. I have seen people who praise God for their own future which clearly states he has no affection for others in this world who are still suffering in one corner of this world, who are not known to you, just imagine in simple logic, if millions did the same God would he have no time to do the required help to each individual, so God already decided his or her future and he knows very well at times they disturb me asking for help, but they don't realize that help is also pre planned by him, it's us who don't know how to handle it, when he can decide your future he decides a mixed future with all necessary qualities in life, it's we who disturb him asking more, because we always want happiness, never ask for it instead be it. There are people who believe God is only in the form of a magician, from the beginning they believe that God is the only person who does magic by giving ashes, assets, money and so on, we humans take advantage of it and we create some magic in front of others and he becomes God and surprisingly people too admit these kind of people as God which encourages them to do nasty things in the name of God.

I am reminded of an incident which happened in my village long back, the people who lived in that village followed a tradition and had a belief that there is God who inside a human in that village, in which that human took advantage of it when he got a chance to react, one day in that village there was a function in one of the temples there and this guy took advantage of the situation and he created a religious drama that God had taken birth in him and whatever the guy spoke everyone started to believe that God himself was speaking ,and from that moment he became popular in that area and he found a part time job being God and after a few days people came to know that in the name of God he started to do nasty things which made that guy retire from that part time job. You know what makes people believe in God in humans? If that human had superhero abilities to bring ashes and assets in the air, so people views on God changed. I do agree that God is inside every human, but he will not encourage a human to make money out of it, he is not a business oriented subject, he stays inside each human to lead our life in a good direction. You don't have to search for God in temples, churches or mosques when he is within you as your unknown master, just try to realize the truth within you.

After first love my wife suffered a lot in her life to overcome the pain, she kept herself engaged by concentrating on her work, but somewhere in her heart she still loved the boy. But she never gave up because her elder sister's marriage was a concern, if not she would have done something stupid, but her commitment towards her family made her live. After her elder sister's marriage she thought her marriage was the only way to overcome her past pain, so she took some serious steps in searching for a groom.

Accidently when searching for a groom she expressed an interest through email, and I happened to get that email.

When I speak about marriage, I have something to express here, according to South Indian culture, when we say arranged marriage, there are some procedures which they follow before marriage, horoscope, horoscope is an important factor which decides a marriage, then comes background verification, that is the groom and bride's family will do a verification from each end to confirm whether the family is good or bad, then the groom and bride's individual likings and finally marriage, if anything goes wrong in the above said points then the marriage is collapsed. My point is where you find love in this is, loves comes after the marriage, but to continue the journey of love after marriage one should have patience, understanding, adjusting and finally to love which makes the relationship pure and long lasting, but I have seen some arranged marriages that are not successful because there is no mutual understanding between each other. A person who continues the journey of love for the purpose of physical requirements or a physical contact relationship, then that is not termed love, that kind of relationship will not last forever. Nowadays, people exploit themselves in the name of love, which should be stopped and people should love knowing what love is.

When I thought to get married, so many of them asked me "Is it the right time to get married?" They said this keeping in mind that we were not well settled, all I had was a job and that too, it is just one year. We were living in a rented house, my father and mother were living with my father's pension, no assets like land, property or business, these were the questions raised to my parents and to me. But I was not bothered at that time, instead I thought I should be honest and tell the bride's family about our situation and the way we lived which made them happy and they agreed to the marriage. As expected my dream became reality after that email, the bride's family never worried about the way we lived, instead they thought their daughter's happiness was important, which made them accept, but for the girl, this marriage was important to show her boyfriend that she too could get a good life without him, because somehow she found that after her boyfriend left her he got into another relationship, which made her very angry and the outcome of that anger was marriage and I happened to fall in that outcome. When the groom and bride like each other then comes engagement to make sure the journey of love continues with full acceptance from groom and bride's parents permission, but after the engagement I had about one full year for the marriage, that one full year is the year, to know, to realize, to understand, to fight, to dream, to plan, to observe, to listen and finally to love each other.

Coming back to the twist in my life, when I was in high school, after that incident, I never took advantage of that, I had a fear in me that again if something goes wrong I would get into more trouble, so I promised to support my friend's love, every year in my school there would be a fete day where the whole school celebrated by conducting games, restaurants, stalls, bakery and so many other activities to make the children happy and get them involved. So my friends said that was the right time to help my friend's love so you will get a chance to speak with the girl. I too agreed to help, the fete day had come, and everyone had the permission to wear colored dress, but to be different from others I wore a uniform even on that day, which made my class disappointed because I was the only one who was in uniform. To participate in these kinds of functions you need money, school does this kind of activity keeping in mind that the school will get some income; the school needs a reason to collect money from the kids so they conduct these kinds of functions. My friends were looking smart with colored dress, what surprised them was my friends girl was also dressed up in uniform, my friends and others started to doubt me, to be frank, I myself didn't know that she would also be in uniform, but everyone thought that we had planned to come in uniform which made my friends angry. My friends in a rough tone asked me, "Today somehow, you should make my friend's love successful; otherwise, you will have to face some serious consequences." The school was crowded with kids' parents, seniors who passed out, friends from other schools, it was a big event and my previous senior crush was present that day. As I said, you need money to play, eat and drink, all I had was two hundred rupees because at that time my father would not give me much money, but the games and eatables were very costly so I kept the money safely without playing or eating, but my friends were spending so much on friends, since I never had that kind of money I was all alone roaming behind my friends without participating in any events. I never wanted to see my senior crush so kept on avoiding her whenever she walked in front, my friends kept on compelling me to talk with my friend's girl, so I finally went to the girl and I told her that I had something to tell her, in return she replied that she too had something to share with me, so I thought this will be an easy task to talk with her about my friend, so I told my friends to wait somewhere till I spoke with her. Ninth grade was into the restaurant since it was her class which was conducting, she took me there. I went and sat inside the restaurant with her and the first thing which I looked at was the menu they had, everything was above fifty rupees. I had only two hundred rupees, if she asked me to buy her something I would have to tell her the truth that I didn't have much money. So I stayed silent for her to talk but she never did that, instead she asked me to say what I had on my mind, just looking at that menu I thought ordering a coffee for her would be a good way to start a conversation with her, so I ordered a coffee, it is just fifty rupees.

I explained to her about my friend and the things hc did to impress her honestly without making stories, but there was no response at all from her end, she just listened to what I was saying to her. My friends came to that restaurant to observe what was happening, at that she took the menu and looked at the items they had and my fear started – if she asked me to buy any eatables I would be in trouble, as expected she asked me to buy a burger, and for a burger the cost is seventy five. My friends observed that she was asking for a burger so they indicated that they would pay for the burger, so I ordered a burger for her. After sometime I asked her, "You said you have something to say to me what is it?" She waited for sometime, after finishing her burger and her coffee she slapped me once again and gave me a letter and left the restaurant. By seeing this my friends once again disappeared and I took the letter and put it in my pocket without reading it, everyone in the restaurant looked at me and laughed once again, and the senior girl who I admired was present in the same restaurant with some other boy, she laughed at me once again. My friends were nowhere to be found, so I thought it's better to leave for home and I was travelling home, when I was travelling in the bus I saw the girl who I had a crush on when I was mid school, she was travelling in the same bus with her friends and she noticed me in that bus and she came to me ask me so many things about studies and about my parents, and before getting down from the bus she too handed me a letter, and with a smile she got down. Two letters in the same day, and the two twists were the content inside that letter. The content clearly said that they both were in love with me. I still don't know what attracted them to love me, later I realized that the girl slapped me because she never liked me talking and helping his friend for love, I admired a girl when I was in mid school which later turned out to be love for some reason, I never admired the girl in high school which also turned out to be love, I was confused about love when these two girls gave me a letter. I thought 'let's not take a decision to love, instead let's see them as friends.' After that incident I couldn't meet the mid school girl, but I was in contact with the high school girl, the whole school came to know about the letter and the content, after sometime my friend realized and congratulated me, but I never told her that I loved her although the whole school thought we were into a relationship. Even teachers used to make fun of it. At that time we never had any mobiles or Internet to converse with each other but I used to write letters to her and in return she used to write letters to me, not love letters just letters. The girl who I admired in mid school never met me after that incident, maybe I should have realized that she chose a wrong guy or she never had a chance to meet me again so that love disappeared after that.

The journey of love continued in high school, everyone was aware of our relationship, since she was a Canadian citizen, her love was just a hobby. I knew it very well in the beginning, that was the main reason I never expressed my love, I waited to patiently to understand what was love from her end, as expected she never continued her love, at some point of time she left me alone, after that I completed my twelfth grade and I forgot all the incidents that happened in school as a new person, I never had any contact with any of my friends because no one liked me, when I was in college I never had anymore crushes in my life. I realized crush and love differs so my entire college life was just a normal college life, I had friends in college but after sometime I lost them at some point of life.

I realized my first love after my marriage, to be frank my wife is my first love, though I admired girls in school or some part in life's journey they were just teaching me what love was, I will never call them first, second or third love, love becomes first love only when you realize what true love is all about, and that true love, which I call first love, is my wife. In everyone's life there is a moment in life where you realize your own mistakes and get ready for a new life, I would say that realization moment in my life was my marriage. Before marriage I never knew my wife had a love story to tell, but at the time of my engagement the girl was telling me that she had a troubled past in her life, which made me realize that the girl was in a state of confused mind. She was confused because on the day of my engagement, the boy who she loved came back in her life once again to admit his mistake, which made her drive crazy, the rest of the situations you can imagine, what confusion would she have had? I realized her true love when she explained about her love and when she explained this I thought I never got someone in my life to love like this, how can a boy leave her? So I thought he had realized his love and had come back to admit his mistake. At that time the very first question which I asked her was "Do you want to rethink about this engagement?" But she agreed to the engagement and the engagement went smoothly, and the best part about the engagement was that the groom and bride were not present, instead my parents and her parents were present and they did a casual procedure of fixing the marriage. We had one year's time for the marriage after the engagement took place, love inside a love started to play its tricks after my engagement.

There was a moment in my life to realize love, likewise there was a moment in my life where I realized God within, this realization took so many years for me to understand what the role of God in our life is. Let me come back to the magic moment in life when I was in Hyderabad, I was away from my home for one year after my grandfather's death. I went back to my home, before leaving there was an incident which happened before leaving Hyderabad. I thought to quit the company and leave home because my interests were to see my parents and to be with them the rest of my life doing some business with them, so I gave my resignation and was ready to leave. After resignation I had to serve the company for one more month, so I waited for one month to get relieved from that company and at the last day after my resignation, I received a call from an unknown number and the person who spoke with me, he said that he wanted to meet me at some place, and there was no second thought that I was going to speak with a stranger. I immediately agreed to meet the person, the very next day I was travelling to my home from Hyderabad after a year.

The magic in my life started when I went to meet that stranger who called me, what surprised me was that the stranger who I met in Hyderabad was a master himself who knew each and everything about me. When he explained this to me I was shocked, how come a stranger collected all my information? He advised me to take the right direction in life, and realize your own mistakes and correct yourself and then he left from there. This incident made me think about my life a lot, the things which the master said was a motivational factor, I asked myself so many times to know who is that stranger to advise me? The next day I reached my home and said this to my parents, I don't know how seriously they took this incident, after so many years I started to believe in God after that incident. After that incident there were so many changes that happened in my life. I started realizing my mistakes which I did in my life, I thought I should help my parents and be with them. I started to develop a passion to drive. So I joined driving school and learned to drive and I learned it very quickly, but I had an inner feeling which made me feel like I already had a passion to drive. When I started something I never used to complete what I started, that's how it used to be, but after the magic in my life I never had a feeling to leave things incomplete. I had a passion to write from that point of time, but I never took it seriously so I just led my life the way it was. I never used take advice seriously even if my parents advised me, I never used to bother about it, but the stranger who I met made me to listen to his advice, and I liked it when he explained with examples. After that incident he often visits me in my dream, but when I wake up I don't remember what was the dream is all about. Driving became my passion, travelling became my interest and I thought writing should be my profession, but that never happened because at that time I was financially not good to publish a book. I started to visit temples, churches and mosques, after that I used to sit silently for a long time and brought peace into myself. All these changes were noticed by everyone in the family which no one believed. All those years I was not a believer but now I am true believer that God exists, which I feel that the magic is within.

Our family got shifted from Tamilnadu to Kerala after my father's retirement from his government job; we planned to settle in Kerala which is our native home. That's where we faced a huge loss when we came to Kerala and finally we ended up here, though working abroad is not my passion, the situation made me work there, opportunities and offers came to me but I kept on avoiding them, even in my life and my career, but somewhere in the corner I wanted to be a professional writer, but never had a chance to write or took a chance by myself to lead to the vision. I did a lot of business and a lot jobs which never made me happy, but two things I know for sure which will make me happy, one is travelling and the other one is writing, but there was no way I could do either without money. I lately realized that my passion is writing and travelling when I met someone who asked me to do this. But at that time my parents never motivated me in these two passions, when I travel somewhere they think I travel unnecessarily with friends, and even after marriage, when I said to my wife that I had an interest in writing she laughed at me often saying, "You will not come up in life with that profession, nowadays even professional writers don't have that much income," that's her point of view, wherein I lost confidence after that. I used to tell my wife I did not want to choose the writing profession for money, but I have an inner passion which makes me happy, when I do what I like, but she never accepted, saying that I didn't have any creativity. I agree writing needs creativity, observation and most importantly passion, if not you cannot do that as a profession. So I never took travelling and writing seriously, instead I did something out of my passion, made my mind fixed to like what I did which made me lose interest in what I did in my entire life. At some point of time I forgot that magic happened in life and the stranger who used to visit me in my dreams disappeared from my life.

Love inside a love is what I observed after my engagement, I knew for sure there will be problems in my life after my engagement, and the trouble was not the boy but the girl who didn't have the courage to say no to either of us. My engagement was finished, when you get engaged what would be your reaction? Obviously the groom and the bride will be happy that they are entering a new life together, I too had the same excitement but the girl was very upset, she was not happy when I was happy which made me think, but I never thought to leave her, my mind was fixed to marry her. I don't know what made my mind think so, I never stepped back. Our days continued with love showers and dew drops, after a few days her mind was again disturbed whether to marry me or not, now this attitude made me think things over, but I never gave up, sometimes she would say she liked to marry me, sometimes she would say she liked the guy who was disturbing her, All these incidents were happening when I was abroad. I stayed silent for a few days, without any reaction. I thought to tell her parents about her attitude towards her life, I never wanted to but after a few months I just gave a hint to her elder sister about it and didn't let her know it, which later turned out to be an issue.

I know all these hints in my life which occurred in life were to avoid her, but something made me stop avoiding her, instead I fell in love with her so much. I am not going to blame anyone for this, we all do mistakes sometimes, those mistake will teach you some facts. Some mistakes will tend you to do more mistakes in life, whatever my wife's mistake was, I never worried because the only problem she had was she did not know how to control her mind and her heart was always frightened. I learned a lot of things from her, I realized what is true love, patience, anger management, how to stop gossiping and so on, it was possible because of my wife. I was not at all worried about her past, though we had lot of problems after the engagement I have always been with her though I complained about her to her parents, I have always loved her. When there was a small dispute between us after a year after marriage everyone thought I was behind her money, that was not the fact, situations pushed me into so called difficulties. My wife had so many problems in the work she did, in her life, in her marriage and with her parents but never had the courage to face it individually. She thinks that her marriage has spoiled her life, but marriage has saved her from all sorts of difficulties. I don't blame her alone; I blame each and everyone who is involved, which includes me as well. In her work she has lost a huge amount, but money is always secondary it cannot be the first important factor in life, which is what my wife thinks. One day she will realize this truth. People have a habit of blaming individuals without even knowing what the reality is because they don't have a good heart, instead of helping they create problems. I will say anywhere that my wife made me realize the good and bad part of life, after one year we are separated for a silly reason which sooner or later she will realize. Let's not get deep into this, that's a whole different story, this whole book is not enough to tell that story, but the climax of the story is marriage so you can imagine whatever the problem is the result is positive.

We have problems in our married life but one needs to understand that problems never create problems, but we create them, after creating them if we sit in one corner weeping for it is not healthy. We need to face it with a mindset to solve it and not to put more pressure to problems that is what happened in my marriage – instead of solving problems we created them one by one. What happens when you create and encourage problems? We get others involved in it, when others get involved that becomes a public issue, when it becomes public, we tend to imagine what others will think of us, so we again create problems so it follows like a cycle, what if we keep silent without reacting to problems? We are on a safer side which is what I did. Me and my wife have faced a lot of problems financially, those were created but weren't with a purpose, it just happened accidently. Me and my wife are not together, that does not mean that we are divorced, but we live separately, concentrating on ours she was the one who said I would not be able to publish my book so I am just maintaining silence without any reaction. I too don't know whether what I am writing will be published or not, but I started writing with a hope and confidence keeping in my mind that one day this creation will be published.

At present, I think you might have read that there was a magic moment in my life when I was in Hyderabad, a stranger who advised me to 'lead your life in the right direction,' but after that I forgot about this stranger in my life. But after that incident I went abroad, step by step me and my family started to live happily, marriage took place, though others were not that happy of that marriage, but we were so happy, some twists and turns happened in my life after marriage but life is still going on and after so many years I happened to see the same stranger who is unknown to me, who I met in Hyderabad once again. I happened to meet him in Kerala, which was my magic moment after my marriage, this magic took place once before marriage and now after marriage. He asked me one simple question this time, "If you see God in front of you, what will be the very next thing that you will ask him or what will be your reaction?" He just asked me this and he disappeared, which was totally a shocking incident for me. I kept on thinking all day, weeks and months, and I am asking the same question to each and everyone who reads this. What will be your answer? At this time I was really upset because my wife was not with me and I didn't have job, and there were so many problems apart from that, but when this stranger asked me this and disappeared I was behind this stranger and was excited to know who was this stranger who was coming and visiting me for no reason. So for days I was engaged with that question to find an answer for that without thinking about other problems in my life. When I met this stranger in Hyderabad, I wanted to ask him who was, he advised me but I forgot, the next time when I saw him I wanted to ask him the same but I forgot, so I was in a mindset to ask this question when I meet him once again. So I was like confused, on the other end my parents and others are telling me not to sit idle instead do something. So I had this question raised within me several times, who is he every day, even in my sleep, as days were moving quick I happened to see that stranger once again and I immediately asked him, "Who are you?" else I would forget so I asked, and in return he replied with a smile, "Why did it take so many days for you to give this answer?" I was shocked, is this the answer for that question? I asked him, "How come this will be the answer?" and he explained.

A person who praises God all day and if God shows up the next thing he will ask to erase all his problems and give him more, a person who utilizes God for his desires and for himself, he is not a true believer, he just praises God to overcome his troubles. A true believer will have no desires for his life, instead he still have a question whether to believe the Almighty or not. God is not a machine who gives you what you ask for, it is already given, all he needs is love and to be loved, a person who doesn't cry in front of him, who doesn't demand anything, who doesn't praise God at the time of difficulty is a true believer.

After he explained this to me I was totally confused because I couldn't understand what he was trying to tell me. I asked him who are you, instead he was telling me who he was, he said something which I never understood, whenever you ask a stranger who he is he always gives an answer by telling his name and revealing his identity, but this stranger was not ready to reveal his identity. I never shared this to anyone I know something different is happening in my life, experiences seem to be new so I waited patiently to know what was happening in my life till I figured out the strangers identity. I know for sure if I tell this to my parents or relatives they will laugh at me, none of them will believe me, if I say this is what is happening in life. Once again I wished to see him to know who he was, why he was giving me advice, from Hyderabad why was he in Kerala in search of me? I had so many questions within, an unknown stranger taking care of my life. Later that night he came in my dreams as soon as I slept, as soon as I woke up I saw him in front of me. As soon as I saw him, with a smile and a very low voice, he said "I am your master," and soon he disappeared with a smile. I was not frightened, but I had a question within, whether he was dead or alive what was he doing in my bedroom, was it just imagination?

As I said, my father is very much interested in astrology so he often meets an astrologer. If there is any problem in life to know the future, not only my father, there are so many others who believe in astrology. If an astrologer can predict your future then he becomes God himself, as far as I am concerned God is the only person who can predict your future. I don't blame an astrologer, he does a good part in his job according to me because those who come to him to know the future he makes that individual happy by motivating and giving good impressions about his or her life. People believe in God, the same people believe in an astrologer and at the same time they believe in humans who act as God and do nasty things. People fluctuate; all they need is happiness so they tend to believe in things which make them happy, these types of people don't believe in God though they say that they believe in God. If you take an astrologer or an individual who acts as God they demand something or expect something, they all need income to or it is just a profession to live their life, God is the only person who doesn't demand anything, it's us who give God, he never likes that either, all he likes is for you to love him and to others who are in need of help, I have seen so many of them spending so much on God when they visit a temple, church or a mosque, they put some money in the box there, but if a beggar comes and asks they are not ready to give or have a heart to give. God does not need your help to survive, but in other ways, in the name of God, there are others who survive, when you think in that way God has helped them by giving a profession.

I am reminded about an incident when I talk about God, after my marriage me and my wife travelled a lot, we visited a lot of places in India, we have covered almost all places in India, since I have a passion to drive a car, I have travelled to all places by car and slowly started to develop a passion as days went by. There is a temple in Kanchipuram which is in Tamilnadu, me and my wife happened to visit that temple which is called the Kanchi Kailasanathar temple which is dedicated to Lord Shiva. When we went inside that temple to see the priest it was not that crowded, this temple was located a little far from the city, the temple is known for its Dravidian style architecture, it has amazing sculptures and statues, and the place is of absolute silence. When we went inside that temple, there are no words to express the beauty of that temple, it was so good, and when you enter that temple you will feel a peace within when you see the main sculpture and Shiva lingam, we met the temple priest there who happened to explain about the temple history, the priest said about a belief which was followed in that temple, there is a passage within that temple where the main shrine is, this passage connects from one side to another side in a circle along with the lingam, an individual can walk through that passage and the belief is when we walk from one side to another through that passage with a belief within seven days there will be a twist in ones life, which is the belief that they have. You can visit this temple for its architectural beauty, after seven days we too had a twist in our life, but at that time I never believed that God was the cause for that twist in my life, but now I agree that's the truth, when you do something with full hope and confidence you will succeed, it's not in God's hands, it's in your hands, leave it to God he knows what to do, just don't demand of him and stay silent, but do your work, he will look into the rest.

God is the power within you, we search for him here and there when he is within you, he is talking to you each and every day, if you keep on disturbing him for each and every thing it means you live your life depending on God, our life is not dependant, our life is how we live ourselves, God has already given you a beautiful life, he already knows how your life is going to be, if you keep on asking for more then how can you listen to him when he talks to you? Stop demanding and expecting, instead listen to him once, he is always calling you, alerting you at times, throw your ego, through your jealousy, throw your desires and start living, listening to your instincts, follow your instinct. I don't know how many of us talk to ourselves when we are alone, think good and positive and then talk to your, own self, you will be directed through a good vision, never mislead yourself with mistakes, if at all you do mistakes try to admit your mistakes and never do the same mistake again, stop looking at others growth, stay happy with what you have. If you have the good qualities within you, in seconds God will be right in front of you, it's none other than you yourself within in the form of God. If you don't have any good qualities then you will have to praise God, but he will not be visible till the end of your life, praise God with love don't praise him with ego. Never be religious just be spiritual.

If a thief becomes a gentleman people don't accept his change, if a rowdy becomes a hero people never accept, if hatred becomes love people never accept, if God becomes a human people never accept, if poison becomes water people never accept, it's our nature that we do not accept reality because we don't believe, instead we stick with the same thing ,which should be changed, when you believe try to accept the life which God has given and don't sit in one corner saying that it's God's mistake, he does good to everyone, it's our view of taking things to reality. The same applies to me here, when everyone saw a spiritual change in me it was hard for others to digest the change in me, because the fact is they don't believe or they don't expect a change when it takes place. I am not worried about it, when you start to worry about all these factors then you will have time to do that alone. There was someone who asked me, "If you become spiritual, will you leave your family life?" family is the reason to become spiritual, without parents you will not be born, without them you cannot be spiritual, they are your source for your life, so how stupid that can be to leave family, see people's attitude towards spirituality, they thought only a sanyasi can follow spirituality, anyone can follow spirituality keeping in mind that you don't follow bad actions. To be spiritual you don't have to avoid your family, instead avoid your negative thought, which is one important factor.

Coming back to reality, after the dream incident the stranger disappeared, the stranger's face is not familiar. I don't remember seeing him anywhere, I started surfing through the Internet to know his identity, but couldn't find him. I don't know his name, either any of his details, all I know is his physical appearance. I thought it's better to share this incident with my parents and I did, obviously they never believed at the initial stage, my father had a little doubt since he reads a lot of books, he thought something strange was happening in my life, so he wanted to clear his doubt so he went to a astrologer to clarify this, he couldn't say what was happening. One thing I realized was that after I met the stranger, I was totally relieved from all of my problems and troubles because before that I was so upset and was not able to concentrate, but he made me engage my mind in one single thing and I was happy, which is what the stranger wanted. You may think, 'why do I keep on calling him stranger?' The reason is he is still a stranger to me. He never showed up after that, for a few days my life seemed to be smooth and good going so one day I went to visit a temple nearby my house, where I happened to meet the same stranger in that temple and this temple seemed to be empty without any priests, I used to visit this temple quite often but that very day the temple seemed to be different with an exotic scene. I couldn't believe my eyes what I was experiencing, I thought all of the things which I was experiencing is just a dream, nothing much, so I went back to my home. I couldn't sleep that night thinking of the incident , my mind was out of thoughts. A human mind is very dangerous, you can't control your mind erasing your thoughts, thoughts are natural, if you don't have any thoughts that means you have no mind, your mind works twenty four seven. The mind plays tricks on you, it will mislead you; it keeps on questioning, it never stops, the heart is the one which answers the questions, it never misleads. I once again shared this experience with my parents, they had no idea, and they thought I might be fooling around.

A short story I would like to share here, a friend of mine who believed a priest would solve his problems went to visit a priest, knowing about this priest that whatever solution he gave for his disciples it would be successful. This priest lives in Kanyakumari, my friend all the way from Kerala, went to visit this priest, the priest is already very popular there. My friend came to know about this by one of his friends who already visited this priest for some problem and his problem was solved, so he believed that his problem would also be solved, so he planned his journey to meet him. His phone was always engaged so he thought calling him would not be possible, let me go meet him directly, my friend has so many problems, let me explain what his problems are so that you can be clear, his problem is his wife, bank debts, kids education, no sleep and money, natural problems that an individual has. So he believed in that priest, that he would be able to solve it by giving a solution for it. The priest had an office of his own, and this guy went inside the office and saw it was so crowded and there was no appointment to meet him. He was surprised by seeing the crowd and thought that his problems would be solved and he would get a solution. Finally he got an appointment after two days to meet him. Meanwhile he just did a small tour in Kanyakumari, visited the famous temple there and after two days he went to his office to meet him. He met the priest and the priest seemed to be very young and smart looking, and this was his profession, so the priest looked at him and asked him, "What problems are you facing in your life," and my friend replied, "before telling you about my problems I would like to share what my friend shared about you and started explaining. Once my friend came here on a tour to Kanyakumari with his family, he happened to visit you at that time, this is what he said, he just explained his problems and you suggested some solution for his problems, and I don't know how far that problem is solved but he told me that you are an experienced priest in giving solutions, so he introduced you to me so I just came to visit you to know how far it is the truth."

The priest was so confused and couldn't understand what he was expecting from him, so the priest asked him once again, "How I can help you?" My friend started to explain his problems and the priest kept on listening and after listening to all his problems the priest asked him his date of birth and his star, my friend asked the priest, "Why do you need my date of birth and my birth star, and he laughed, the priest said that he wanted to check how long the problems were going to continue, so my friend gave his date of birth and star. The priest did something, he whispered some mantras and after a few minutes he said, "Your problem will continue till so and so year and the solution is ..." and he said offer some money to so and so temple and the problems would be solved. My friend thought for a while and again asked the priest about his married life, the priest immediately said, "After some years your married life will be so good beyond your imaginations," and he continued with so many offerings to different temples and his problems would disappear. This conversation went about an hour with so many offerings and so on, but my friend was not satisfied, he asked the priest, "How come you are suggesting me to do so many offerings? What guarantee is there that my problems will be solved after I do all the offering which you have suggested?" The priest said, "First do this offering and then come and visit me, if the problems are not solved." So my friend asked, "You are very sure that I will come and visit you once again, which means it is just a test to know whether the problems will be solved or not, am I right?" The priest thought that this guy was so annoying and he thought, 'I should somehow make him leave this place,' and he created a drama in front of my friend, that God had come inside his body and that God wanted him to go out from this place and don't keep on annoying God by asking unnecessary questions. My friend asked him, "How can I trust you that you are God? For proof take something from air and show me." The priest took some ashes and threw them on his face, my friend was shocked by seeing this and he apologized to him and he left that place paying the money. When he reached here he told me that there was a priest in Kanyakumari who was an expert. Now reading this what do you all think about the priest? Was he an expert, no he was marketing his profession, he was creating publicity, from the beginning people are cheated like this in the name of God, whether it is an astrologer or a priest, he is spoiling his own life, and thousands of others life too because he knows nothing about his life or others' lives.

When my friend explained the scenario, I thought he was so courageous and he would not believe in all this stuff, that is how he explained the story, but at the end, he too behaved like a normal human with small magic. There are so many people out there who act as God in humans to make others believe that he is God's own son, and once people see they want to know what God has showed up, what message does God have? Is it Lord Shiva, ram since Hindus have so many gods they keep on asking which god has showed up, people actually cheat in the name of God, it is far better to spend for someone who is helping others in the name of God, but don't help someone for his own growth in the name of God. The priest took ashes from the air because he was an expert with that trick. I don't know why my friend believed that, our problems' solution cannot be solved by someone else, we created our problem only we can solve it. If you have bank debts that's your problem, if your life has problems that's your problem, if you don't have a good married life that's again your problem, and the solution is within you for all the problems. Giving money to some priest and others will not be a solution for your problem. God is a solution for your problem, don't tell your problems to him, he already knows them, why do you keep on reminding, he has given you those problems to overcome and face those problems individually. Just believe in God and praise him with love.

All these years, I have grown up hearing stories about different gods in our religion, different religions follow different customs and culture, but humans are all the same and equal, though we are separated with religions and cultures at our hearts everyone of us is equal, love has only meaning and all religion has only one God, which I realized very lately. I agree knowledge is power, but God is the source of our knowledge, what if God decides to create humans without mind, so what is the point of knowledge, knowledge becomes power only if you have the mind to grasp that power in you, else knowledge remains powerless, knowledge is not permanent, at a certain age people lose their memory, what happens to the knowledge you gained?

God is the source to knowledge which makes it powerful, and God is love which is permanent, God can create humans without a mind but he cannot create a human without a heart, he creates humans full of love, if a human does not have a mind can grasp if you show love, the heart will accept that love, the next second that's the power of the heart, all God needs is love. I have a friend who is well known in his studies in schools and colleges, and even in his career life, his knowledge is extremely powerful. If you ask him any question he is ready to answer, he will never say that he doesn't know anything, he is so intelligent. One day he met with an accident and this guy with that accident, he lost his memory. He could not even recognize his own parents, he forgot all his memories. I still remember when I went to meet him in the hospital, he was just totally blank. I heard the doctor telling his parents that he needs love and care, apart from that there is no other way that you can bring him back to normal, knowledge is good, but ego with that knowledge is not good, God decides something what we cannot even imagine, always keep in mind that the source of knowledge is God, be happy with what you get, face past problems with happiness and accept live problems with happiness.

If you look at my book, from the start till the end the experiences which I had will always be incomplete, that's how our life is, it is not complete, and you become complete only when you throw away your ego, till then your life will have ups and downs, happiness decides your ups and downs. How can you stay happy all the time, which is a very difficult task according to humans? Happiness showers in the form of love, only love can make you stay happy, by listening to comedy speech, watching a comedy movie, reading a comic story, all these things can make you happy just for few hours, but to stay happy all the time is not possible because on some occasions you cannot be happy, but you should not be carried away, you can bring back happiness, it's in our hands to stay happy. I was happy but life never allowed me to stay in that stage for a long time, I too had the situation where my happiness was being tested, it's how you accept that situation with a bright face, you need to control your emotions in such a way that you will not be carried away with your past and future emotions. Present is what we live, so stay happy with what you live for at present, if one can admit this truth he can always stay happy, a person who thinks about future and past emotions and incidents, then he will not be happy, however you try to change him.

I happened to read an article long back, it was just an imaginary story, they just used that article to convey a message which I would like share with you too. There were two friends with their family and kids, they were staying in the same colony, their friendship was an everlasting friendship from kids they were friends and still continued to be the same life long; they were well settled, were in good jobs, life was going on smooth, if a friend bought something, the next day the other friend also would buy the same, they were so close, they never had any secrets and they were very honest with each other, both were very religious and worshipped Lord Vishnu. Both of them spent so much time with God doing mantras and praying. One night, one of the friends had a beautiful dream which made him so happy, he dreamt that Lord Vishnu came into his dream and blessed him, saying you and your kids are blessed with happiness. So this guy was so happy as soon as he woke up he wanted to share this excitement with his close friend, so in the middle of the night he called his friend and said, "This is what I dreamed," and he slept that night with happiness, but the other friend, though he appreciated him, he was not convinced and that night he lost his sleep and happiness. From that night onwards he was totally disturbed thinking so many things, because this guy could not accept his dream, it's not because he never believed his friend, it is because his ego never accepted it. He too, praising God the same way he was praising but God had not come in his dreams, why has God not appeared in his dreams? After that incident his attitude changed and every night he slept expecting that God would also come in his dreams, which never happened, but his friend was so happy in his life, and this guy lacked happiness and jealousy started to form, the friendship started to collapse, happiness faded away. In simple terms, accept others' happiness without any grudge, and don't spoil your own happiness by seeing others' growth which is not healthy. When others are happy join their happiness and learn to appreciate them full heartedly.

The stranger never appeared in front of me for a few days, but my attitude towards the outside world totally changed. I am not a nature lover, but I started to admire nature and get involved in the beauty of nature. I felt that nature was talking to me, trying to express, felt peace within, I myself couldn't believe what was happening to me. My parents couldn't believe that I changed a lot, I had a lot of problems at that time, but all of a sudden my house turned out to be so silent. My thoughts about past and future totally disappeared, I could feel happiness all over, whenever I felt happy within I got carried away with nature. There were no second thoughts, I never knew what made me change so. I started loving the outer world, I never bothered about spending the time all alone, I maintained silence free from thoughts and enjoyed the real happiness within. Then I slowly started to realize the incidents which happened in my life, I knew all the incidents were somewhere connected and there were hints to follow life which I never took seriously at that time. It took this many years for me to understand the truth within. I started writing about the incidents which happened in my life, when I wrote the incidents that is the first time I recognized that these incidents were connected or were trying to give me a hint to follow towards my passion, which I never did, now I came to know with a help of a stranger. I will not call him stranger, instead I will call him my master.

When we say master, a master is an expert, full of experience, a master is out of ego, a master full of love, I will not say he is God himself, instead I will say he is full of godliness. A master will teach only what is required in our life; if a master misleads a student or a disciple he is not true to himself to be a master. A master will not tell himself 'I am an expert', it should be observed by others, he speaks through his heart and his eyes in the form of silence, silence is not an enemy, it is pure love, and you need to learn how to be silent. When I talk about silence I am reminded about a story, I hope everyone knows who Ramana Maharishi is, at the beginning I too never knew who this man was, when I surfed through the net I happened to see his photo, when I saw it I got a sparkle within like electricity passed all over my body, this man is the man I kept on calling stranger. I was stunned for a few hours and my eyes were filled with tears, then I happened to read his Wikipedia and came to know that he is the real master; he is a master of silence, that was the day when I started to believe in spirituality. That is the story of how a stranger turned out to be a master. He was the only one who provoked me within to do self enquiry within to wake up the real master who is unknown to you all these years, an unknown master within through meditation. Meditation is an adventure, adventure into the unknown; it is the greatest adventure the human mind can take. It is just to be, not doing anything, no action, no thought, no emotion, you just are, it is a sheer delight, the delight comes from nowhere, or it comes from everywhere, it is uncaused, existence made of the stuff called joy. Meditation is nothing but the discovery of inner sense.

After realizing this truth, I explained this incident to my parents and others, though my parents believed, others never believed, so I thought it's not necessary for me justify, one thing for sure they believe in God only when God comes in front of them or sometimes they will not believe in God even though he himself appears in front of you like me, to be frank I never believed. I still have confusion, the reason is I still have a doubt whether all these incidents are just imagination. People who believe in God definitely will believe the incident that is the real fact, all these years I have never thought about spirituality or I never thought of praying or doing meditation; I started meditating from the day when I realized that God wants me to understand the real meaning of life.

Now readers may have so many questions within, obviously this is something which is not that easy to accept, I too never accepted, but as days travelled I started to observe a change in me which made me believe, you may have a question, "How did I conclude that the stranger was Ramana Maharishi?" I never concluded, but time concluded it. My father is a bookworm, he used to read a lot of books based on spirituality, so when I explained this to my father, he believed it in the next few seconds and he started to explain about the master who was enlightened, that was the first time in my life I had heard a word called enlightenment, meditation and enlightened masters which made me surf through the net about all the enlightened masters – that is how I came to know Ramana Maharishi, else I would not have recognized him. We say miracles happen in life right, but we don't know when that so called miracle will happen, wait patiently it will happen to you as well.

When I started meditating, everyone was against me, mostly people believe meditation is done to control our mind and free from tension and stress, not only that, if you meditate seriously there are so many things which you can observe within you, you have travelled outside the world, for a change let's travel within and explore the adventure within which is what meditation is all about, anyone can meditate, it's not an easy task, if everything becomes easy their life will not have any meaning, different masters follow different exercises in meditation, follow your comfort level in meditation, it is something which should be observed without a master, a master is just an add-on to make it perfect. Your life has a vision and a mission, the same applies to meditation, when you meditate you should have a vision as well as a mission, you become oneness. My vision is to wake up my master who is unknown to me within, my journey within started and I am still on my journey.

I will praise the God within. I will not search for him in some other place, instead he is all over, observe the master within to know who is God, reveal your identity, reveal your purpose, reveal what is required in life and finally reveal the truth within.

Do you know the master within you is shouting at you when you commit a mistake? He is trying to tell you what is good for you, he trying to give you more knowledge about yourself, nowadays who has time to spend some time staying alone? Even though time permits, your mind does not permit, you are always scheduled, you are always trying to keep yourself engaged with different works and get overloaded with tensions and stress, your daily routine and your body follows what you have taught your mind, so it becomes a habit and you end up saying that there is no time. Why so much tension and stress in our life? the one only reason is money, everyone is behind this factor, I too agree you need money, but why do we need more? if God gives you more and still you demand more, if you have more just give to someone who is actually in need of it, if you demand more make sure you demand for others, not for yourself, let others live happily with you, this kind of mentality is very rare among us, if this mentality is followed our country will have no poverty, our country will be free from poverty, there is no love, there is only lust.

Love and God, there is nothing different, both are the same, if you have love \god follows you, when I say love it's not only within your circle, everyone in this world, you don't have to go to each and everyone and express your love, instead you can sit where you are and can express your love to them, what is wrong in that? If you have enough money try to help others. This is what all religion and all books say, we know all these facts but we don't implement all these known facts. If you ask someone to talk about it they will talk, but there will be no reaction. I have never taken love as a serious subject, though I haven't taken it seriously I haven't mislead my life in the name of love, because I never knew the real meaning of love, when I started to believe in God within I started to realize what love is. Love shouldn't turn out be a revenge game, it should be only love, don't worry how others react when you love them, just accept life with love, love is for the ones who deserve it, as well as God is for people who actually deserve his love. Let's imagine a world full of peace with no poverty and everyone is equal, imagine a world full of love and prosperity, a world full of happiness. Love is more powerful than God, you can even make God fall for you with the same love, and to love you should lose your ego. In order to lose ego, you should throw away I in you, I is very dangerous, and ego never lets you share your love to others, it will only look for your happiness and not others. God created this world out of his love, this world flows out of his love; it is his expression and an explosion of love, we are all protected with his love, we all should become beloved to God, once this love penetrates deeper within the heart, the love will transform within and to the whole being, your inner darkness vanishes and you become love. This energy is perfectly healthy; we people have one problem within when we think about love, people don't listen to their inner voice, people should experience the inner voice. Don't be distracted by anything else, follow your own feeling, if you are happy, be happy, if you are sad, be sad, don't consider others, their expectations, your energy is flowing perfectly, since you consider others too much you get carried away, which should be avoided. Nobody is here to fulfill others' expectations, and people who do that will always be in misery which is my personal experience; this means an individual is not true to his own self, he loses his own respect, which means showing disrespect to God within. Respect yourself, which does not mean disrespect others, try to be soft on yourself which automatically transforms the same to others as well. So when you start listening to your inner voice, try to be committed, if at all you have to go against others expectations, try to be polite with them, apologize and don't pretend, This is one of the problems that always comes in relationship: you have to consider the other, continuously, and he has to consider you, and both become false, inauthentic. How can love grow when both are inauthentic, insincere? Love grows in authenticity – it is a fragrance of authenticity. One needs to be absolutely genuine, only then does love grow. So in the world there are so many lovers and no love at all, because the basic requirement is never fulfilled. I started to recognize this fact after years, the moment which I call realization, understanding, believing and being spiritually involved.

Love can be formed out of meditation, which is what I am talking about. If you meditate sooner or later you will come upon love, when you meditate seriously you will start to feel a tremendous love inside you that you have never known before, a new quality within you have never experienced, you have become new and you want to share. If you love deeply you will become aware that your love is becoming more and more meditative. Love makes you meditative and at the same time meditation makes you loving. Just love, which is born out of meditation, not out of your mind, millions of people around the world are living as if love is there, they live "as if" obviously how can they be happy? False love is being created and they get something else out of it, so frustration, boredom, nagging and continuous fighting between the lovers. This love has come out of your mind; the mind cannot give you any glimpse of the eternal. First, go into meditation then love follows you. In meditation silence is understood to be something negative, empty, an absence of sound, this is wrong, very few people have ever experienced silence; their view of silence is noiselessness. Silence is positive energy, it is not empty, it is overflowing with a music that you have never heard before, the joy you have never experienced before, fragrance which is unfamiliar; it can be witnessed only through your inner eyes. It is the reality and it is a reality which is already present in everyone, we just don't look into our inner world, it has its own taste, fragrance and own light. Lives come and go, days come and go, ages come and pass but the eternal silence within you remains the same because you are it. Anything which you do can be a meditation, if we keep alert in our daily activities and get into oneness then every act that you do is a meditation, it is not something you sit and face east chanting some mantras, people think in that way, but the real fact is you automatize what you do.

When we talk about Ramana Maharishi, there was a time I called him a stranger, but now I call him the real master who made me think of my life, my passion and most importantly to be spiritual. I was totally inspired by his teachings; he was the one who made meditation to ask and to inquire "Who am I?" And don't believe in any answers which the mind supplies, though the mind gives you answers like, what nonsense are you talking, I am a man, I am a woman, I am rich or poor, I am educated or uneducated and so on, the mind keeps giving answers, but don't try to accept any answer just keep on inquiring asking questions because the answers which are given by the mind are false answers, these answers are from the unreal part of you, these answers are coming from words, from society, from others, from the things that you have experienced, just keep on asking within, let this arrow of who am I penetrate within deeper and deeper, and there will be a moment when no answer will come. The moment of answer, because the mind is becoming silent, or you are gone far away from the mind, when there will be no answer then a vacuum will be created all around you, your questioning will stop, those answers were of the mind, both have dissolved, so now you are. He was such a great soul, enlightened master who was so successful with his teachings, when I recognized the stranger in my life I began to praise the God within, meditation is an art you have to understand then you will not be able to come out of that art. He was the one who taught the cause for love is happiness.

I am reminded about an article which I read about love, written by another great enlightened master Osho, I love his teachings on love, he is not just a master he is beyond imagination, to be frank I seriously never had an idea about any enlightened masters, but God gave me an inspiration to look and observe so many things. The life before spirituality and the life after spirituality is what I am in this book, I started realizing love only when I started believing that God existed within. He tells very clearly that love is not only termed as relationship but it's a state, one is not in love but one is love, he tells that relationship is good but that relationship becomes false, if you don't attain that state of love, then the relationship becomes dangerous. Love never arises just by falling in love with somebody you like, love arises only by going within deeply, not by falling but by rising, soaring upwards higher than you. Love makes no conditions, no ifs, no buts, love never says fulfill these requirements, and then I will love you, love is like breathing, when it happens you are simply love, it does not matter who comes close to you, the sinner or the saint, whoever comes close to you will start to feel the vibe of love, love is unconditional giving, but only for those who are capable of giving. I too agree with the above factor, how sweetly and perfectly he has explained about love, relationship is just a structure and love is unstructured, love is a moment to moment process, it is a clear state of our being. There are people who are lovable and who are not, people who don't love pretend to love through relationship. Love needs no relationship, love is enough. Relationship happens one day and disappears another day, it is like a flower which blooms in the morning and they are so bright, and in the same evening it is gone, just be a lovable human being. This is a difficult task which cannot be followed, so in the name of relationship they just get involved in love, it is a kind of security financially or something else, it acts as a substitute.

I recognized my passion was to write, passion is like tying a knot, when you tie a knot to it you have a chance to get bored after a while, our interests cannot be our passion, though you have a passion, try to be passionless. Same with love, if love becomes a passion then love is like a hell, don't get attached to love then you become arrested, and you will feel like that you are in a prison. Passionless in love, and love without attachment makes love more precious because you have the freedom and there love becomes the divine energy. I don't mean that you cannot have a passion or attachment in love, but it's like skipping your freedom to love, when your love is pure, innocent, formless, when you give in love and don't demand, when love is only a giving, when love is an emperor, not a beggar; when you are happy because someone has accepted your love and you don't trade love, you ask nothing in return, then you are liberating this so called love into the open sky. Love has made people fall low and even rise high, it all depends what you have done with love, and love is a mysterious feeling, the inner heart has two sides in love, one is suffering or hell, and the other is freedom or bliss. Love which becomes devotion, which becomes prayer, which becomes attached, will seem like just a play of words. You have also known love, you knew love full of passion and attachment, love is not real; love is just a curtain to hide the passion, attachment and sex. Love acts as a decoration outside and inside it is something else, it is natural that a man or a woman who are in love long for sexual relationship, so love is just a factor for that longing. I have also in love but I got back only misery, in the name of love we are creating a seed of thorns within, which is more dangerous than explosives. People say that they fall in love, or fell for the girl, my point is where did you fall? Fall from where; love is rising from within, it is a falling feeling from the mind to the heart within. Falling in love is falling from mind to heart in love. Love becomes more, it expands, it grows so we reason love, and love is not reasoning, it is blind. When someone asks what the meaning of life is, he lacks love in his life, so he finds life meaningless, if love is there, there is no question of life. Life is not meaningless; love is the real meaning of life. All my life I thought my life had no meaning; our existence must have a meaning, we all do our daily routines everyday, waking up every morning, working till evening, sleeping in the night, the same pattern is followed in our daily life and we follow the same until our death, so what has happened? Love has vanished; love has its value when you live your life with it. Fill your life with love so you will be out of fear, everyone in this world is longing for love like children, people need love, so they long for it, expecting that one day he or she will be showered with love, you need love from everyone you see, that is your longing, but you cannot want for love, love is only giving, marital life faces this problem in love, couples live their lives longing for love or expecting love from each other, and they lack love because they don't have a heart to give, but they need love in return, if you have a heart to give without any expectation then that is love.

My entire life was totally involved in love, but I never understood the real meaning of it, I always longed for love rather than giving, I have always expected, I have always feared all these qualities can be voided if one thinks and understands the real meaning of love. Ego is a disease, it is a cancer within, ego drives you ill, it will never allow you to relax even for a second, if your life becomes more and more miserable, then you are travelling towards ego and you become an egomaniac, but love is just the opposite, for an example, if you like a girl and you want to express your love for her, you have to fear because you don't know the other side of her, she has her own ideas, she may think which may create issues and troubles, sometimes you get complicated thinking all these factors, love yourself to throw this fear from you, if you cannot love yourself you cannot love others, when you start to love yourself your vibe of love can be seen through others. When you love yourself there is no outer world, it's only you within, there is no other disturbance, it is your pure silence, and the pleasure is unexplainable. If a person is capable of loving his own self, he will be capable of sharing his love with others as well, no doubt in it. You can only share things when you have to share, the same applies with love only if you have love within, only then will you be capable of sharing it with others. A person who is greedy of money, he becomes that money, he loses spirituality, never love wrong things, love things which can make you reach higher depts., which give you more joy and happiness, remember to be in that state permanently, love transforms very quickly, it is like electricity, whenever you love something you are transformed to that thing, instead of loving the wrong things which lead you nowhere, believe in God, show and share your love with him then there is no turning back or falling down, you can stay happy. Love towards assets will not be permanent; at the same time love towards love (God) is what is permanent. Nothing is so transforming than love, it is something beyond you, experience the adventure within to feel the inner peace. If your life is becoming happier, tranquil, silent, joyous, together then you are travelling towards the right direction of love. Life's journey can be explained through ego and love, if you follow ego your life will be miserable, and if you follow love your life will be blissful. Ego tries to destroy, whereas love makes you survive, when you move towards love, ego will disappear, but ego plays tricks on you, it pretends to be self love, it is very cunning and very self justifying, and if you are not very alert it can rule over love. So the very self will start to protect the ego, and ego will start saying that I am your own self. Then ego turns out to be a fantasy, so in order to take away the ego within, you need to be very alert that ego should not rule yourself, and give way to love to rule you. Self is God, and our real reality is our self.

Life needs happiness, and most importantly life needs love, as humans we are not satisfied in whatever we get, we ought to get more and more and that's what a human's mentality is all about, you cannot make them happy, you cannot make them love, you cannot make them understand, one should experience all this. From the beginning of our life we have to cross different stages, right from a kid to an adult, we are taught by others the essence of money right from the kid, parents when they grow up their children, they never feed them love, instead they feed them the requirements in life. I agree money is essential, but money never decides our lives, we decide our lives. We don't know about our own potential, parents cannot be rich, so they want their kids to fulfill their ambition, so as a result parents pressure their kids, and kids without knowing their ambition they get into something because of their parents and make their life miserable. Some professions will not earn you much, which is why most of the parents wanted their kids to be engineers, doctors and so on. If we go in a direction without knowing our potential we will be a failure, to become rich don't throw your inner secret, even though if you become rich throwing your inner secret, you will continue to face the difficult even after you become rich. Follow your inner emotions and inner ambition because nature has already designed your life, try to grab the ideas about what your inner instinct asks you to follow.

After education, the next thing is career and then marriage, mostly marriages in India are done based on birth charts which is absolutely stupid, you can see with these marriages, how well it is going, birth charts are just a tradition or culture that we follow, my point is, how many of us are happy with these kinds of marriage? Marriage is not decided through birth charts it is decided with love, I have seen so many of them in my life who keep on consulting a palmist or an astrologer about married life, kids life and our life comparing with stars, stars have nothing to do with our life, stars never decide our lives, mostly people in India follow this belief, which make people's lives more miserable, and creates more fear within so we are into so many superstitious barriers in life, education is necessary in life, keeping in mind that an individual has the ability to become what he likes, else education will not support, maybe it will support him to become rich, but he cannot live a joyful life. As I said, life is a journey from the time you are born till your death you should keep on travelling, experience the love within when you continue your journey.

I think many of us will have faced loneliness, how many of us would have thought loneliness is an enemy, yes it's our enemy because you feel that you are sitting in darkness, you feel loneliness because you are dependent, do you ask your own self why this loneliness is caused, you will get an answer, and that answer is your first step to avoid loneliness, and that very step is nothing but love, ego which pretends to be self love will give you this so called situation loneliness, because the love was not real. I too have faced this situation, but at that time I never knew what the real cause of loneliness was, but I used to ask myself why I feared this loneliness. Is loneliness our mistake? Yes it is an opportunity given by God to think about life, to be an observer. There were three friends, two of them were fighting with each other, and the other one who was very clever just witnessed the fight instead of stopping it because if he joined the fight or if he gave advice at that moment, there would be more problems. He knew nothing about the fight. If you get involved you will be transformed to that fight and you become that fight and the other two will put the blame on you, never get involved in anything without knowing the real fact, it is far better to witness. The same applies in life, just witness what is happening around you, just be an observer, most of our life is spent living for others, rather than our own life we care about others, but do you know whether others do the same? Every one of us cannot be the same, different people have different views about life, let them live their lives accordingly, understanding the true nature of love. Loneliness became my friend, when I was alone thoughts came up, everyone is frightened of these thoughts, because if the thoughts are miserable then you tend to run from that, no one accepts the thoughts, instead they get into it and expand the thoughts, which should be avoided. Just witness the thoughts and stay silent, don't disturb the thoughts which come up, if you disturb the mind starts to question it, leave the thoughts as they are, after some time you will stop questioning. Once the mind stops travelling then you are entering into an adventure world, you will start to experience the inner world full of love, loneliness and silence is the first step towards the journey of love within. Don't be frightened of loneliness, try to overcome loneliness and start to love your own self.

If you ask a kid to draw the symbol of love, even a small kid will draw the heart-shaped symbol; the symbol itself says that the heart is the sign of love. I would like to share about Ramakrishna Paramahamsa here in brief, another enlightened master who is an example of love. On 18 February, 1836, a child was born at Kamarpukur near Kolkata, in Bengal. This divine child was destined to return to Hinduism the glory it had enjoyed before the foreign conquest of India. The child was named Gadadhar. He later grew to become Sri Ramakrishna, as a child, Sri Ramakrishna showed wonderful qualities of purity and love. He loved the company of Sadhus. When he was nineteen, his elder brother, Ramkumar, appointed him priest of the Kali temple at Dakshineshwar. His love for the Mother grew beyond all bounds. To him, she alone was real and the world became a mere shadow. He poured his soul into his daily worship and longed to obtain a vision of the Mother of the universe. Sometimes, in agony he would rub his face against the ground and weep bitterly. Such was his longing to obtain her vision. He reached a point when his agony was so great that life held no more meaning for him. It was then that he had his first vision of the Divine Mother. He was then initiated into Vedanta meditation by Totapuri, a reputed monk who attained oneness with God after forty years of penance. Such was the devotion of Sri Ramakrishna that, to the amazement of his Guru, he attained in one day, what the Guru took forty years to achieve! In his very first sitting, he remained absorbed in the state of Samadhi or God-vision for three days; he was unique in every respect. He was a living image of godliness. Some may know about this great master, but obviously our new generations will have no idea about all these people, so I thought I would share something which I know about the great spiritual master. He passed away in the year 1886 due to throat cancer. Nowadays, people don't have time to remember all these great souls who were a living god once. But his teachings haven't disappeared. These people should always remain in our heart, they are the very first examples of love. I don't know how many of us read about their articles or show some interest to know all these facts, I don't tell everyone to follow spirituality, spirituality is for the ones who believe in oneself, but there is no harm in knowing things, which is what I would like to convey here.

Meditation has to become a habit in our daily life, like other habits in our day to day life, you don't have to give much time for it, whenever you have time, just sit silently doing nothing, just witness what is happening, I happened to visit Ramanashram after knowing the truth, to explore more about him, when I went there I was so hungry and it was early in the morning, since it was an ashram I thought those who came to visit the ashram, they provided breakfast too. It was my longing to have food in that ashram so I asked the person who seemed to be well dressed, who was inviting others to the dining hall for breakfast. If I am not wrong, he was the supervisor, so I went and asked him, "Can myself and my parents have breakfast, is it possible?" He never even smiled at me, he said breakfast is served only for those who stay there, I am not blaming anyone here, that might be the ashram rule, according to God whether it be an ashram or a house, if someone comes and says that he is hungry and he needs food, you need to have a heart to give to those who need it, that is where godliness is seen, ashram was so silent and beautiful, that was the first time ever in my life I visited an ashram, because I had no idea about this master and no idea about spirituality, suddenly I had a vision of a stranger in my life, later I recognized who the stranger was and why I had such a vision in my life. In my life I have seen him without even knowing who he was, now I totally regret my mistake, I realized that God is with us, he is everywhere, but we never recognize. He is always with you, but we are not with him, he reminds you, but we don't remember, I would not believe in God if this master hadn't taught me, I would not have known him if the master would not have reminded me, miracles happen in everyone's life, but what did you learn or realize from that miracle? A miracle happens to lead life in the right path. The master was very clear, he did not want me to follow his path, he just reminded me to follow my path, which I lately realized. I have explained this incident to my parents and my family members, I was least bothered whether they believed it or not, but I felt very happy and even my parents felt very happy, my parents couldn't believe the change in me, but the one thing I clearly said to them, the vision which I had is for good, there were reasons why my parents believed, they had never seen me running behind spirituality or even being religious, they had never seen me so silent, they had never seen reading books, they had never seen me talking about masters who I had no knowledge about, though my father read a lot of books he was stunned hearing me. I am not a follower, I am not God, but I am inspired which is what I explained to my parents. I felt a change within, my lifestyle is changed, my thoughts have been changed, my point of view towards love has changed, looking at things have changed, all this was possible because I started to meditate, God made me realize the importance of love and I am still continuing my journey of love within.

My experiences in life as well as in love are worse, people pretend to love each other, people are running behind time, they don't have time to do anything, the world is moving so fast with no time, so people are tied in all aspects, they don't have the liberation or freedom to sit in silence even a second, mobiles are another factor which people are behind, people may forget God at times, but they will never forget their mobile, mobiles are their love of life, even I too had mobile, I stopped using it for a long time, though I used mobiles I never used to get carried away with it, nowadays people find it very difficult to live without, if you ask them they will have so many excuses, it has its own advantage and disadvantage, but one should never be that object. People are transformed to mobiles, if you can do it just try to put God in the place of a mobile, you don't have to do prayers or you don't have to praise at a particular time, whenever at your busy schedule. If at all you have time, just sit in silence witnessing, love to God will be formed. So many of them asked me, "Are you going to leave your family and wife?" If I do that then what is the point about love? They were my stepping stones to love, I cannot leave them, God is not so cruel to tell someone to leave his family and follow his path, all he says is to love him like you love, you love others. It is not necessary that you should love only your family, share your love with everyone, which is what God needs, share your love with him, without demanding and just by giving, the way people think is wrong, you have the freedom to do anything, it's how you utilize your freedom. If someone is into spirituality the very next thing that they assume, is he going to be a sanyasi? Those who follow that they follow, there are so many masters who are married, let's create a world of enlightened souls, let's create a Jesus, let's create a Krishna, what is wrong in it, it's an individual's freedom, God has never said for anyone to be this or be that, but he says to lead your life in the right direction without harming and hurting others. Marriage is not a burden to follow spirituality; spirituality becomes more after marriage because love is more. There are people who think if a person can materialize things from the air, he is the real God, no one can do that, maybe a magician can do, spirituality is not magic, it is an art of love, materializing objects, making others believe by doing some magic tricks is not godliness, godliness is helping others and loving others without any ego and treating everyone as equals which is real godliness.

Money, which is essential in life, money is like the heart, you cannot survive without a heart, the same with money, but money should not be our goal, my troubles and problems in my life are money, no one is against, there is nothing to say against it, it is a good means, but it is very dangerous if you don't utilize it in the right way, never love money, don't let money to rule you either, you cannot buy love or happiness with money, money is just a factor to live life, it has nothing do with happiness and love, society is circulated with money, so are we. Don't get obsessed with it; instead of loving money let your soul love yourself. When money flows jealousy is born, jealousy is born out of comparison, as adults no one has to teach us to compare, others have a big house, others have money, others have a car, he has a good career, he has a better body, he has a better life, we keep on comparing with others and the result is we are jealous. If you stop comparing then jealousy disappears, out of jealousy life becomes very complicated and miserable, why create a hell out of jealousy, just be yourself and stop comparing, happiness follows in the form of love. You know how people get diverted, their mind is not fixed on one single thing, it keeps on wavering, why do people enjoy sleep? Your mind stops thinking, when thoughts arise you are depressed, don't get diverted, let that depression happen, depression becomes complicated only when you don't allow it to happen, let it happen and free yourself, depression will disappear by itself, for that matter it can be any type of emotion, let it happen, don't try to rule it or control it, let it happen, you can experience the real freedom in you. Why do you trouble your body for your own emotions ,just let it free and see the change. So many of them asked me what if thoughts arise during meditation, just witness the thoughts and don't fight over it, thoughts will come and go just stay witnessing it, meditation becomes easy only when you accept, else meditation is meaningless. People who cannot love others start loving money because money is a means to possess things. The more money you have, the more things you can possess; and the more things you can possess, the more you can forget about others. You will have many things, but you will not have any contentment because deep contentment comes only when you love a person. The money will not revolt but it cannot respond also, that is the trouble. That's why miserly people become very ugly. Nobody has responded to their love ever. How can you be beautiful without love falling on you, without love showering on you like flowers, how can you be beautiful? You become ugly. You become closed. A man who possesses money or tries to possess money, is miserly and he will always be afraid of persons and people because if they are allowed to come closer they may start sharing. If you allow somebody closeness, you have to allow some sharing also. People who love things become like things dead, closed. Nothing vibrates in them, nothing dances and sings in them, their hearts have lost the beat, they live a mechanical life. They drag, burdened, burdened with many things, but they don't have any freedom because only love can give you freedom; and love can give you freedom only if you give freedom to love. People who are afraid of love become possessive about money. People who love become non-possessive, money doesn't matter much. If it is, it is okay, it can be used; if it is not, that too is okay, because love is such a kingdom that no money can purchase it. Love is such a deep fulfillment that you can be a beggar on the street and you can sing if you have love in your heart. If you have loved and you have been loved, love crowns you, makes a king of you. Money simply makes you ugly. I am not against money. I am not saying: 'Go and throw it away,' because that is another extreme. That is also the last step of the miserly mind. A man who has suffered too much because of money, who has clung to money and could not love anybody or become open, becomes so frustrated in the end that he throws away the money, This man has not understood. If you understand, money can be used, but people who don't understand are misers, they can't use the money, or they renounce the money, because in renouncing they are also saving the same mind. Now there will be no difficulty in using it: you renounce all and escape. But they cannot use the money, they are afraid of using it. You can accumulate money, and then one day you understand that you wasted your whole life in earning that. When you understand this you become afraid, you can give the whole and forget about it and escape, but you cannot share it._If a man of understanding has money he shares it because money is not for itself, it is for life. If he feels that life needs it, love needs it, he can throw it away completely, love is the goal for him; money is never the goal, money is the means. For people who are after money, money is the goal, love becomes just a means. Even their prayer is for money; even prayer becomes a means to money. Our ego feels much fulfilled with the money, so people are so much into it, money is like a magnet, it can possess you, but you cannot buy love with it. But people go on looking for money as if money is going to bring happiness. People go on looking for respectability as if respectability is going to give them happiness. People are ready, at any moment, to change their pattern, to change their ways, if more money is available somewhere else. Once the money is there, then suddenly you are no longer yourself; you are ready to change. Don't be just abnormal, be normal understand the world, live life in understanding and observing things, you will be healthy, God has created such a beautiful world outside, enjoy the beauty of it, experience your inner world and wake the unknown within. After marriage I have faced a lot of difficulties in life, but I have always taken life as a burden, laziness is my friend, I enjoy staying happy all the time. I had so many problems only after marriage, I have faced and experienced depression, stress, ego, jealousy, love, money, marriage and finally love for God. Life before marriage I, never had that many problems so I never took my life that seriously, after marriage I started to realize love within which turned out to be a different direction in my life, I don't expect anything more from anyone, but I still feel how come I missed a master? I just kept on avoiding because I was not that serious about life, at some point he made me realize what life is. I will say this is a miracle, this may be a miracle or a surprise for others, but for me nothing has changed except my attitude. I am still a normal person.

I have even thought that God was just an imaginary character; that he was not real, when I felt that it is totally wrong. I couldn't figure out how a person with a negative attitude could suddenly change to positive. This is where I feel the miracle lies, the miracle is not the master, the miracle is the change within and the master was just an inspiration. There are so many people out there who have so many visions, which never make any difference; the difference is how far you have realized your own self after that vision. For the first time, when I sat for meditation it was so difficult for me to fight over thoughts, but slowly I started to observe what meditation is, what love is and what life is. I am far behind from enlightenment, this is just the beginning of a new era in my life; let me experience it myself, which is what I feel a miracle. Though I don't believe in God, I am happy to know that God believed in me, he believes in everyone; let's just form love so he can come to us in the form of love. I actually felt fear only after marriage, and then when I started to meditate, I realized that fear is so stupid, why should we fear for no reasons, people fear of illness, old age and death are ordinary fears, it is natural by birth, fear for no reason, makes you real scared, because we don't have the courage to face it, we start imagining things which makes you fear more and more. Fear is an experience in meditation, just interrogate going deep into it, just watch and witness, you can overcome fear. When you are asleep, dreams can be of fear, dreams are just mind tricks, and dreams have no meaning. We should be able to experience as many things in meditation, just witnessing should be our vision and never be scared to experience, everything should be experienced, when you experience you become mature, just accept and get used to it. So make this fear your meditation. And the mind will ask again and again 'Why? What are you afraid about?' Don't listen to this question; that question is dangerous. That leads you into more and more verbal explanations; a distraction from the fear. Just go into fear itself, with great love for this experience. If trembling arises, tremble; if you feel shaken, then shake. There is no need to hide it, and the society which has made you very much of an expert in these things. Love is God, This is the ultimate truth. But let me say as well that love also exists within the family unit. This is the first step on the journey to love, and the ultimate can never happen if the beginning has been absent. Love is responsible for the existence of the family, and when the family moves apart and its members spread out into society, love increases and grows. When a man's family has finally grown to incorporate all of mankind, his love becomes one with God. Without love man is an individual, an ego. He has no family; he has no link with other people. This is gradual death. Life, on the other hand, is interrelation. Love surpasses the duality of the ego. This alone is truth. The man who thirsts for truth must first develop his capacity to love – to the point where the difference between the lover and the beloved disappears and only love remains. When the light of love is freed from the duality of lover and the beloved, when it is freed from the haze of seer and seen, when only the light of pure love shines brightly, that is freedom and liberation.

A friend of mine asked me, "What is the difference between arranged marriage and love marriage." I asked him, "Why do you have a question like that, I asked are you married," he said no, then why did this question arise? I asked him another question, "Are you in love?" he said yes, "Do you trust your girlfriend?" he said no. I asked him, "Why don't you trust her? What is the point telling me that you are in love?" he said, "When I fell in love I forgot to think." I asked him, "What would you do if you had a chance to think?" "I would choose a better girl." I said, "Now you have come to the point, the freedom is yours, but don't spoil the relationship in the name of love, love needs freedom, only then can you love, why do you think about marriage if you don't know how to love?" So the question of marriage becomes effective only when love is genuine. A few months later when I saw him again he said he got married, I congratulated him, I never asked anything, he himself told me that he got married to the same girl, "After you explained to me about love, I realized that love is not pressurizing others, it is our freedom to trust each other." See love can grow in you when you act mature, when you start understanding, when you observe the truth. Everyone's life has some or other misery or some secrets within, just overcome it with love. I have seen people suffering in love, a friend of mine attempted suicide twice in the name of love, why imagine to that extent, why do you act in that way, is suicide a solution for love, if that is the case ninety nine percent of us would have already been dead, no one asked you to show much sincerity in love, without even knowing what love is, there are few others in the name of love, they spoil others' happiness, so many end number of incidents. I have a few others who fall in love after seeing a movie, people try to live with movies, change their lifestyle accordingly, I will not blame that but just see cinema as a mode of entertainment, don't try to live with it, a movie is making your mind engaged in oneness for two or three hours, wherein that three hours your mind will not think about anything else, why can't you take the same practice in meditation, I do not mean not to watch movies, at the same time I just want you to think if can make it possible for meditation as well. If you take movies, there is an option, if people think they do not want to go and watch in theatres, they can watch on television when it comes, or through a disc, but to read a book, there are no other options. You need to get a copy of it, no other choice, reading books is a good habit, you are not only developing your mental skills but you are totally out of thoughts if you get involved in it, for that matter you can read any books, whether it be a novel, fiction, thriller, spiritual or any other genres it's up to you.

A few years back, in Chennai, I went to a small tea shop in the early morning to have tea, I happened to be the first customer early in the morning. I ordered a tea and waited patiently to get served, I had my tea and I asked him how much and he said seven rupees. I gave him the money he required and I left for home. The next morning, I visited the same tea shop again to have tea early in the morning, this time it was a bit crowded and as usual I ordered tea and gave him the money, when handing him the money he said he needed no money. I asked him why, he said "Keep it with you sir." I said "I am paying you for what I had, there is nothing wrong in it." he again kept on compelling me not to pay, so I asked, "what is the reason you are not accepting the money?" he explained, "Usually my tea shop will not be very crowded, maybe on weekends I earn some money, that too it is very doubtful that I will get profit out of it." So I asked him "Why do you tell me this?" He again continued, that when I visited his tea shop for the first time yesterday, I was the first customer to have tea in his shop, and I was the first one to give the money, and this guy believed that since I paid him first in the morning, the whole day went so well and he earned some profit that day. On hearing this I began to laugh, I gave him the money and I said, "That was your belief, maybe yesterday you might have been so happy, so business gave you happiness, it is not at all my luck, it is your happiness within, don't believe in others just try to believe in your own self, happiness will follow." I told him money shouldn't be your happiness, you became so happy when your business gave you profit, never be like that money is not happiness, others' happiness should be your happiness, even then he was not convinced. I told him I would come to this shop after a week and "All I want you to do is to be happy in what you do, let's see what business gives you." He too agreed and after a week he realized that his love towards the business gave him happiness, likewise understand what is our joy and try to implement in what you do you become that joy.

People in this modern age have been taught to become successful in life, there is a lot of effort required, effortless cannot make a man successful, effort is success, we struggle, we fight, we focus and at times we get hurt, there is a lot to do to be successful, but what you get out of it, the more you face life with these qualities you become more tensed and stressful and life becomes so difficult and you finally want to escape from life. We need to be aware, how can you be aware? It is only possible if you have a mindset to relax, meditation can be a solution for this, but in this modern world no one has time, so it seem to be difficult, people are relaxed when they watch a movie, when they go on an outing with their family, when they are with their family members, but my question is, are you relaxed? Acceptance makes us relax instead of fighting with life, accept life as it goes, which makes life easier without any difficulties. If you have a heart to accept then you have a heart to love. I am not going to give techniques on how meditation can be done here, meditation is understanding, you need to experience it yourself, though you have teachers to teach until and unless you read you will not be able to understand, meditation is not a technique, meditation is an experience, you can't feel when one says that, one who explains the experience, remember that he is sharing what he experienced, once you experience it may differ. People watch movies, but opinion or reviews will not be the same, it differs from people to people, the same with meditation, though the meaning and concept of love remains the same, views will differ. If you take spiritual masters, everyone speaks about God and everyone believes that God exits, but their point of view on God differs. There was a disciple who went and asked the master, "Does God have a structure?" Structure is what we created, God is within, and the structure is your own self, we need to create godliness within, when Jesus said God is love, you will not be able to understand it, it is pure godliness within and godliness is love. Different enlightened masters follow different styles and views to express the feeling of love, so their vision differs, when love increases within for a single object, then you become that, your self possess that godliness, like Ramana Maharishi believed in Lord Shiva, so he had that vision, the same with Ramakrishna Paramahamsa, he believed that mother universe is his love and he had that vision, so it depends with all other masters, God is only one almighty power, and that power is within us, we are God, like I said, we can create godliness within with love, that is what spirituality teaches us, love can take us beyond limits, love can show us visions, though you don't believe in God, you believe in love, you will get visions of love which is what I too experienced in my life.

Life is already designed, you are born without any expectation, expectation starts when you grow, our freedom is limited within the family and the society that we are into, when our freedom is limited even love becomes limited.

When love becomes limited you will be limited to share your love for others, you have your freedom to love yourself, no one will come and ask you not to love your own self, if you love others then there will be questions whether to love or not, when you have your freedom to love yourself just love, so when you understand love, it becomes more vast then you will not hesitate to give, giving is loving. Thoughts are unlimited in a human mind, thoughts are very natural but questioning thoughts is a misery, when questioning stops thoughts will not cling to mind. The mind is controlled and you will start experiencing, let me not get deep because the next is the adventure of love within, you alone have to experience.

I had a question within which disturbed me all the time in my life, can we receive God's love through prayers? Why do we pray to God and for what reason do we pray. I have seen everyone praying, there are people who feel prayer is the reason to reach God. Prayer is not useful which the real fact is, religions have been teaching people that prayer is a means to God. It is not! Prayer is God. It is not a means towards anything, we are the divine, and prayer will not lead towards the divine energy, you want God, you want to grab God; now you are finding ways and means to grab. And God cannot be grabbed! YOU cannot possess God. You cannot contain God. You cannot interpret God. You cannot experience God. Then what can be done about God? Only one thing: you are within. Nothing else can be done about it, God is within you, recognize it or not, realize it or not, God is within. And only that can be done which is already there; only that can be done which has already happened, nothing new can be added. The mind has so many questions and it keeps on asking why, though you control again the why starts. So the first thing to understand is: Drop questioning, and suddenly the energy moves in a new dimension: the dimension of the heart. The heart has no questions, and there hides the answer.

When I slowly started to follow spirituality, I was so much impressed by the teachings of the great philosopher Osho, I haven't read all the books which he has written but some of them I have read. I happened to observe his teachings and his styles of explaining things in a very sweet manner, he is known for his yoga and meditation techniques, he is a true master of love. I have never come across anyone in this world who taught about love in depth, he has so many followers all over the world, everyone in this world knows about him, he has written over six hundred books in his entire life, and he has read around sixty five thousand books in his entire life, which is another record, he was a professor in philosophy, he was known as Chandra Mohan Jain and later he was known as Bhagvan Shree Rajneesh and then later he was known as Osho, the great mystic guru and a spiritual teacher. My father is also one of his followers, he is known for his spiritual teachings, he is another enlightened master and very much different from the others.

Before turning out to be spiritual, to be frank I was a person who raised questions about God and love. I am a normal person, even now I am the same, but the change in attitude is the only difference, my idea is not to give or tune you towards spirituality, tuning others into spirituality is not the right way to bring others into it, you cannot give others a choice, but people have the right to choose, that's what the freedom is talking about, people at some point of life will have a chance to self realize, spirituality is not something that seeing others and you try to imitate what he is trying to do. One should realize his own self, this happens only when one thinks about it, no force, or no actions or no teachings can make others change, change should happen naturally, if you force someone to follow then that is not the freedom, you are actually diverting his mind to follow what others follow. Likewise, you see a movie and in that three hours if one can change his attitude, then change is not real, that is the excitement which a human has at that time, apart from that there is no other change in him. If you see any romantic visuals we tend to do the same in our life, which is not healthy. Healthy is to be holy, prayer will not make you healthy, the same with meditation and also with love, these are some good qualities which a person can follow on his own, this is not something forceful to do. It is something like in a classroom you will have different students with different mindsets, but you will not know how many of them are mentally present or mentally absent. If a teacher can observe that then the teacher is an expert, but it is not possible, if a student is not alert then you cannot force him, if you force he will lose interest, a student who is interested will not lack alertness, he will try to observe and experience things, which is exactly what I want here. I don't need anyone who is alert and aware; instead I am much more interested in conveying a message to those who are not alert, not in a forceful way but naturally. How can it be possible, through love, if a teacher tries to convey a message to a student? Obviously a student will have so many questions within, but the teacher should have the patience to answer the question. If a teacher hesitates then teaching is a void. Likewise love is the master in life, if love never develops then life is void and the master remains dead, when love forms life is active and the master keeps you alert, here the master is self and self is love and love is life. I am not a master or a teacher I am just an observer through experience. When I say experience, it should be observed, you can observe only when you are alert, how can you be alert and aware, only if you are relaxed. From the time of my school I have been asked so many times what is my ambition and what is my goal, when someone asks me this I tremble because I don't know what it is, some say they have so many ambitions and goals in life, it is just a play of words, we are not the ones to decide so. The decision should be made from within, therc are some people who chose with a mindset, whether to choose or not. Some take a strict decision and lead to that vision, some succeed and some may not succeed, it depends, my point is whether they are happy or not, if they are happy then well and good, no second thought, if they are not happy, rethink what made you unhappy. We are the mistake and we are the solution for the mistake, it's our own self no one else can give you a solution. One of my school friends had a vision to be a doctor, he worked very hard to be a doctor, but that expectation was totally collapsed when he never got a seat for doctor, so he tried another year but was not possible, they were not that financially sound, this is how life is, you cannot expect, if you live with expectation then your life will be full of misery, if you have the courage to face the misery then proceed, else stop right there and live a life without any expectation.

Why do people go on comparing? Because they don't have any other work other than comparing, people will never avoid loose talk, once there was a rich man and a poor priest, the rich man was very much a god-fearing person, he believed the priest and he liked his teachings, this priest lived in a village, where this rich man happened to visit this priest every week. If at all there was a function or any festival, the rich man used to consult with this priest for all occasions, whenever he came the priest would get enough money, when this rich man entered the village everyone looked at him with so much respect and even the priest, the priest was very friendly with the man, the village never had a school so the village people gathered in the priest house for a favor, the whole village said somehow we need a school here so if the rich man can sponsor some money for the school it will be better for our kids future, so they said this to the priest, first the priest never agreed because he knew very well if the rich man said no, then their friendship would lose its value, so first he never agreed, later when the village people kept on saying this the priest thought that they are asking for a good cause, let's ask him, he is so rich definitely he will help, expecting that he would travel to the place where the rich man was staying. When he went inside the house he saw the man was praying so loud, asking for more money and happiness in life even though he had so much money, by hearing this the priest went to him and said, "I came here to ask a favor from your end, though I came to beg for a good cause, you are begging God for more and more money, though you have so much money. So you are still a beggar." The priest smiled at him and left the place. People need more they will not stop begging, they will always beg in front of God, do you think God will help you, he never likes demanding he already gave you enough, what else do you need in life? He has given you a good heart to love, why don't you give him love? and how can you expect something from him.

Everyone of us knows who Buddha is, but here is something from my end, he is another one of the great enlightened masters. As a child, Siddhartha the Buddha was troubled by some of the same thoughts that children today have. They wonder about birth and death. They wonder why they get sick and why grandfather died. They wonder why their wishes do not come true. Children also wonder about happiness and the beauty in nature. Because the Buddha knew what was in the hearts of children and human kind, he taught everyone how to live a happy and peaceful life. Buddhism is not learning about strange beliefs from faraway lands. It is about looking at and thinking about our own lives. It shows us how to understand ourselves and how to cope with our daily problems. His father was King Suddhodana and his mother was Queen Maya. Soon after Prince Siddhartha was born, the wise men predicted that he would become a Buddha. When the king heard this, he was deeply disturbed, for he wanted his son to become a mighty ruler. He told Queen Maya, "I will make life in the palace so pleasant that our son will never want to leave." At the age of sixteen, Prince Siddhartha married a beautiful princess, Yasodhara. The king built them three palaces, one for each season, and lavished them with luxuries. They passed their days in enjoyment and never thought about life outside the palace. Soon Siddhartha became disillusioned with the palace life and wanted to see the outside world. He made four trips outside the palace and saw four things that changed his life. On the first three trips, he saw sickness, old age and death. He asked himself, "How can I enjoy a life of pleasure when there is so much suffering in the world?" On his fourth trip, he saw a wandering monk who had given up everything he owned to seek an end to suffering. "I shall be like him," Siddhartha thought. Leaving his kingdom and loved ones behind, Siddhartha became a wandering monk. He cut off his hair to show that he had renounced the worldly lifestyle and called himself Gautama. He wore ragged robes and wandered from place to place. In his search for truth, he studied with the wisest teachers of his day. None of them knew how to end suffering, so he continued the search on his own. For six years he practiced severe asceticism thinking this would lead him to enlightenment. He sat in meditation and ate only roots, leaves and fruit. At times he ate nothing. He could endure more hardships than anyone else, but this did not take him anywhere. He thought, "Neither my life of luxury in the palace nor my life as an ascetic in the forest is the way to freedom. Overdoing things can not lead to happiness." He began to eat nourishing food again and regained his strength. On a full-moon day in May, he sat under the Bodhi tree in deep meditation and said. "I will not leave this spot until I find an end to suffering." During the night, he was visited by Mara, the evil one, who tried to tempt him away from his virtuous path. First he sent his beautiful daughters to lure Gautama into pleasure. Next he sent bolts of lightning, wind and heavy rain. Last he sent his demonic armies with weapons and flaming rocks. One by one, Gautama met the armies and defeated them with his virtue. As the struggle ended, he realized the cause of suffering and how to remove it. He had gained the most supreme wisdom and understood things as they truly are. He became the Buddha, 'The Awakened One'. From then on, he was called Shakyamuni Buddha. After his enlightenment, he went to the Deer Park near the holy city of Benares and shared his new understanding with five holy men. They understood immediately and became his disciples. This marked the beginning of the Buddhist community. For the next forty-five years, the Buddha and his disciples went from place to place in India spreading the Dharma, his teachings. Their compassion knew no bounds; they helped everyone along the way, beggars, kings and slave girls. At night, they would sleep where they were; when hungry they would ask for a little food. Whenever the Buddha went, he won the hearts of the people because he dealt with their true feelings. He advised them not to accept his words in blind faith, but to decide for themselves whether his teachings are right or wrong, then follow them. He encouraged everyone to have compassion for each other and develop their own virtue, "You should do your own work, for I can teach only the way." He never became angry or impatient or spoke harshly to anyone, not even to those who opposed him. He always taught in such a way that everyone could understand. Each person thought the Buddha was speaking especially for him. The Buddha told his followers to help each other on the way. How many of us see Buddha as a role model, very few, I have heard people saying often that their role model is a celebrity, a sport star, football player, hockey player, singer, people who are rich, but very few respect people like Buddha, why can't Buddha be a role model, why can't Ramakrishna Paramahamsa be a role model, why cant Osho be a role model, but people's views about life are entirely different, once even I was the same, but now I understand my mistake.

No one can escape death and unhappiness. If people expect only happiness in life, they will be disappointed. Things are not always the way we want them to be, but we can learn to understand them. There is suffering, suffering is common to all, and we are the cause of our suffering, stop doing what causes suffering and find a path to end suffering, this is the known truth, Being honest brings peace into the world. When there is a misunderstanding, the best thing is to talk it over. This precept includes no gossip, no back-biting, no harsh words and no idle speech; do not seek happiness by making others unhappy. Focus on one thought or object at a time. By doing this, we can be quiet and attain true peace of mind. No matter what we say, others know us from the way we behave. Before we criticize others, we should first see what we do ourselves, we are what we think. Clear and kind thoughts build good, strong characters, by speaking kind and helpful words we are respected and trusted by everyone, a worthwhile life means doing our best at all times and having goodwill toward others. This also means not wasting effort on things that harm us and others. To end suffering, one must cut off greed and ignorance. This means changing one's views and living in a more natural and peaceful way, people do things that are harmful to their bodies and peace of mind, so they cannot be satisfied or enjoy life. The things people want most cause them the most suffering. Of course, there are basic things that all people should have, like adequate food, shelter, and clothing. Everyone deserves a good home, loving parents, and good friends. They should enjoy life and cherish their possessions without becoming greedy.

"Faith, faith, faith in us, faith, and faith in God – this is the secret of greatness. If you have faith in all the three hundred and thirty millions of your mythological gods, and in all the gods which foreigners have now and again introduced into your midst, and still have no faith in yourselves, there is no salvation for you. Have faith in yourselves, and stand up on that faith and be strong; that is what we need. "Why is it that we three hundred and thirty million people have been ruled for the last one thousand years by any and every handful of foreigners who chose to walk over our prostrate bodies? Because they had faith in themselves and we had not." This was said by Swami Vivekananda.

As per Mahavira, his way of teaching was entirely different, he followed three rules in life, which is right faith, right knowledge and right conduct, he clearly explains all these three rules and how we are connected to it, let's see in brief.

The right faith is perhaps the hardest of all. Nobody can tell us what we can believe, but we can look at the message of Mahavira and believe that he really did know what he was talking about and that his message makes sense. Mahavira's message contains the basis of right knowledge, life is a puzzle. Where did we come from before birth? Where do we go after death? Nobody's life is completely and totally happy, but why do some people have lives of great misery and others have much joy? Mahavira teaches us that this is not the result of the whims of some distant god. No, each one of us is what we have made ourselves by our actions in this life and in previous lives. Every individual (and not only humans, but animals and plants) is basically a pure spirit or soul which is capable of complete knowledge and complete freedom. But by our actions and thoughts we have, as it were, covered this pure spirit with the gross material of karma which obscures our knowledge and limits our freedom and ties us down to one life after another. Although we may have a lot of happiness in life, we also, all of us, have a great deal of unhappiness. We want to know the way in which we can get rid of the restrictions of karma and gain the state of complete knowledge and glorious freedom which is known as moksha or nirvana. Although this may be a very long, very slow process for most of us, over countless lives, Mahavira teaches us how to make a start in freeing ourselves from the restrictions and miseries of karma. So we come to right conduct. Strength of passions is the worst thing, passions of violence and desire and possession. The most important principle which runs through the whole of Mahavira's attitude of life is ahimsa. This is usually translated as 'non-violence', but it goes beyond that and really means the greatest possible kindness to all living things. This is the first and fundamental rule which we should try to follow, to get rid of violence in all our actions and even in our thoughts. Yes, in our thoughts as well, for violent thoughts can be potentially as harmful as violent deeds. Mahavira's teachings, if faithfully followed, have two results. Firstly, they produce a better society for every creature to live in, and secondly, they enable the individual to improve his or her own inner feelings and character. So, following on from ahimsa, we are taught to be truthful and honest, to create both individuals and a society in which lies and theft, and general insecurity, are absent. Lies and theft are the result of our passions and possessiveness. True peace and harmony in society and in the individual are possible only if we can restrain our passions and desires. So Mahavira tells us to reduce our longing for the things of the world, for material possessions and for sexual activities. We can never have real peace of spirit so long as we are constantly seeking more and more possessions and pleasures. These then are the five rules of conduct which Mahavira taught, non-violence, truthfulness, no stealing, non- acquisition and control of sexual desires. It is a hard program and not everybody can follow it all at once. So Mahavira set up a society in which some people, monks and nuns, try to follow his program as far as is humanly possible. Others, ordinary lay people, men and women, do not give up their homes and jobs and families, but they try as far as possible in the circumstances of daily life to follow the five rules of conduct. While the monk or nun can take precautions to avoid harm even to the tiniest living creature, the rule of non-violence must mean something less for ordinary people caught up in the ordinary business of our lives. A monk or nun can give up all possessions and seek no more: for most of us non-acquisition must mean trying to reduce our craving for possessions and the pleasures of the world. Monks and nuns can go very much further than married men and women in subduing their attachment to sex. Mahavira taught his message for thirty years until his life on earth ended and he passed on to that state of complete freedom and bliss and peace which we call moksha. For most of us moksha is a very long way away. But he taught us how we can approach it ourselves by rules which lead to inner peace and harmony inside ourselves and outward peace and harmony in human society. He taught more than that, a democratic organization in the society which he set up, with all men and women playing their part and with no barriers of class or caste. He also taught tolerance and an appreciation that things can be seen from more points of view than one. Above all he taught that we ourselves produce our own fate by our own actions and emotions: we should not look outside for some god to praise or blame or ask for favors.

In this age, known as Kali Yuga, Buddha, Mahavira, Christ, all the saints and sages, have said that the form of religion should be love and compassion. Being compassionate, loving and kind towards others was the teaching of these sages for this age. However, what would the teachings have been in another time, in the past, when people had a different kind of lifestyle and were living according to the precepts of dharma? The relevant teaching for that age, as enunciated by Krishna and as enunciated in the time of Rama, was involvement with karma. Rama did not say to be compassionate; it was part of the natural expression of that society. There was no poverty, everyone had plenty. There was no need to become charitable. People were charitable, compassionate, loving and kind by nature; it was part of their personality expression. Today we are not charitable, loving and kind by nature; we are by our nature creating an egocentric and self-centered society. So, the teachings have to change according to the time and the mentality of the people who form a society. In the times of Krishna and Rama, when there was affluence everywhere, when there was no rampant poverty, when adherence to dharma was an integral part of the human act, there was confusion as to whether to renounce action for the attainment of God or whether to involve oneself in action. Rama, and the teachings that Rama was exposed to, spoke about acceptance of action and living according to the demands of the situation. Krishna, and the teachings of Krishna, speaks about accepting and realizing action. This idea is the underlying philosophy of life as practiced in those times. In the Bhagavad Gita, emphasis was given to acceptance, performance and realization of actions. It is also said that knowledge of action, knowledge of human participation in life, in this creation, understanding the role that each human being has to play, is a very secret subject that has never been revealed before. But it is only through perfection in action that one can improve the quality of life.

Teachings which bring God closer have changed accordingly time to time, though the concept remained the same different saints and sages followed different paths to convey the same message, involvement of love remained one hundred percent in all ways, the new enlightened mystic Osho is a true light and inspiration for any radical seeker in the world today. His main teaching is about freedom, love, enlightenment, and how to heal our lives from the inside out, though the thoughts were different, everyone followed the path to God in the form of the reason. Why I gave some examples of other masters is to understand what the master tried to convey, if you look at the teachings you can clearly say that love is the first and foremost factor which they tried to explain. Generations might have passed, ages might have passed, years might have passed, but love remains the same, whether it be old age or new age, love has always been so important in our life, love is the basic necessity for life, love is the first step to adventure life, without love life is empty, no fragrance, no music, no joy, no happiness, life will be a total misery. Travelling life with love and with the unknown master within makes life more easy and comfortable, don't look at this as a teaching, just try to look this as an experience, when you look at the mirror and you see your own self what would be the first question that arises in your mind? Nothing else but the source of I within. Who is this I? The answer lies within, experience the answer, observe the answer and understand. Let's have a look at what Ramayana and Mahabharata convey at that age; they were the real superheroes in ancient history. As per the teachings of Ramayana, whatever may be a person's academic distinctions, he cannot, by his wisdom and self-education alone understand the import of the several doctrines and the purport of numerous incantations, embedded in the sacred works. Such an attempt may even lead to a confusion of his thoughts. It requires a spiritual teacher to unravel the mysteries and explain why several restrictions have been placed, even in the matter of religious pursuits. For instance, Valmiki says the life of one who has not seen Sri Rama or on whom the Lord has not showered His grace, is not worth living. Is it then possible to have a vision of Sree Rama? Answering in the affirmative, there is a song which says, if one threads a royal road of devotion, without anticipating immediate returns, there is bound to be everlasting bliss. Sri Rama will protect his devotees like the eyelids safeguarding the cornea, enabling them to conquer the three foes within, the uncontrollable mind, the impure body and ignorance.

Shortcut methods to seek Divine blessings are there no doubt, but they are like by-lanes. Incarnation of God implies His descending from His abode to the world, donning the garb of a human being, why should He adopt this step and what is the necessity? are the questions that may be asked by this. God provides human beings with a rare opportunity to rise to the level of Divine creation. God lends a helping hand to lift a sincere person and give him the necessary wherewithal to turn himself into a Divine being In His incarnation. God demonstrates how this can be achieved He will act as a human being, but will not be susceptible to sentiments, nor be affected by grief or other weaknesses It is not God's intention to take us directly to Heaven, but He points out that by following the norms He had set in His life, a person can outshine others by developing certain distinguishing Divine trait. No one is born with such outstanding qualities, but in the course of one's life, one can acquire them. The essential requirements for such a distinction are adherence to the principles of righteousness, respect for Moral Law, reverence to truth and submission to justice and whereas Mahabharata is considered, The author of the Mahabharata, Sri Bhagvan Vyasa talks about the sufferings of the Pandavas and Draupadi, Nala and Damayanti, Savitri and Satyavan, this clearly explain to us the fact or hard truth that the goal of life or perfection can only be attained through pain and suffering. Pain is the means through which man is molded, disciplined and strengthened. Therefore, one should not be afraid of pain and sufferings. They are blessings in disguise. They are eye-openers. They are silent teachers. They turn the mind towards God and instill mercy in the heart, strengthen the will and develop patience and power of endurance, which are the pre-requisites for God-Realization. The message of the

Mahabharata is the message of Truth and Righteousness. The great epic produces a moral awakening in the readers and exhorts them to tread the path of Satya and dharma. It urges them strongly to do good deeds, practice Dharma, cultivate dispassion by realizing the illusory nature of this universe and its vainglories and sensual pleasures, and attain Eternal Bliss and Immortality. It induces people to do what Yudhishthira did and abandon what Duryodhana did. Stick to Dharma tenaciously. You will attain everlasting happiness and Moksha, summon of life.

We have heard of this story often, right? From our grandfathers and your parents narrating to your kids? But, how many times have we plunged into the meaning that this epic has to deliver? Why did Laxman leave all the luxuries of a palace and join Rama and Sita on their grueling 14-year long exile? The answer is simple … love! He loved his elder brother Rama more than anyone else. On the other hand, when Rama's cousin brother, Bharat learned that his mother Kaikayee had sent away Rama on exile, he was devastated. Why? Need I have to give you the answer? Yes, it was love! Bharat's devotion towards Rama was so great that when Rama refused to return from exile. The world we live in today is very materialistic. We are always in need – for wealth, power and status. Where is love in all this? Disputes and rivalries among siblings is nothing new, is it? People need to be encouraged to love others around them … parents, grandparents, teachers, peers and even animals. They need to learn the principle of standing by each other when in need and fight for individual freedom and freedom to others for love, when I say love here I am not encouraging false love which makes your own life miserable, what I mean here is love in sharing things, love your own self, understand what love is, never beg for long, don't long for sexual relationship in the form of love. Love isn't an object, God isn't an object, both have no difference, it is just an energy within our own self, try and understand how that energy within is formed, I don't encourage or motivate to be spiritual, it is something which an individual should try to understand, but understand that spirituality is a natural feeling within in the form of love, but we don't look into it or try to observe. I don't blame people who are devoted or worship God, it is the individual's point of view. I have no right to say don't worship, worship God but remember that you don't curse him or blame when your life is not blessed with happiness and love, the cause for that is you, your own self and the solution is you, so why blame God for it, which is my point here, your problems and mistakes have a remedy, I will not say meditation is a remedy or becoming spiritual is a remedy, but I would definitely and one hundred percent say that acceptance, truthfulness, prayerfulness, love, happiness and following your instincts (listen to your heart, not your mind) is the one and only remedy for all your problems, there was a person who I know used to say all the time that he had so many problems within mentally and physically, and he could not overcome it; do you think there is a remedy or solution for these problems? No not at all, the solution lies within and for a human mind to accept it takes much time, we know for sure that we are the cause for our own misery in life, then why don't we accept that truth, why do we keep on finding excuses and why keep on blaming God, when you were born your life was new to you, you see things, you hear things, you observe things, now your mind works in such a way that it will take all the rubbish and all the good stuff, the mind is confused, your ego is activated and your heart is filled with all this rubbish, now can you tell me do you have a space within to know where love lies, where godliness lies, when you approach God telling your problems, which means your life has lost faith. If your life is miserable and you start to hate your own self, you want to run away from this world, which means you have lost love, and when you don't know what to do when life becomes miserable and you cannot accept or find a solution or happiness in life, which means you lost your life. I have seen people praying for life, money, status and joy, but they forget that their life has all that is required, but the way they have been brought up in the society is what matters, it's easy to blame others I agree. The question is not blaming, the question is we live our lives the way others live, because we don't worry about our life, we live our lives worrying about how others live their lives, so there is no question of love there, there is ego and jealousy, love cannot have these two qualities, without these two qualities is what love is all about, then that is the place you go beyond to build up a divine energy within which is so much joy and no words to explain that inner feeling. People cannot disagree that they don't love sex, sex is natural, everyone will accept, if sex can be natural, why can't love be natural, why cant godliness be natural, why can't spirituality be natural? Which is what I am trying to convey here. At a certain age we try to understand and observe what the role of sex in life is, though you have been taught in school through science, being a man and woman we try to understand it ourselves, we don't have any questions related to it, though you have questions, you don't have the courage to ask because we feel that is a secret. Most of the parents are not that open-minded to share things when kids grow, there are a few things which parents should teach their kids at a certain age, else the kids in the name of love they will be exploited, which is what is happening in this world. Sex is not something that should be experienced without any knowledge, it is something pure, in love sex is a factor, but longing for sexual pleasure is not love, before marriage knowing about sex is not love, after marriage knowing what love is and sharing love with each other with a true understanding is what love is all about. Sexuality and spirituality are two different things, though both involve love in it. The question is where love exists, of course love lasts forever and exists only in spirituality, in sexuality, love will disappear as soon as the pleasure is lost. Imagine if a boy or a girl develops love, slowly in love the human mind tends to long for sex which is quite natural, because the mind which has grabbed the knowledge about sex transforms within the body, where the heart of true love is avoided, they only think about the physical pleasure where they tend to forget love, and sex becomes the core factor which should be totally avoided, attraction towards physical beauty should be avoided, and going deep within inner feelings about love and sex will be a void, it will be just love there, when the heart speaks there is no way that physical contact can happen, pure love is formed. Respect your own self, realize the truth, follow the right path without harming or hurting others, love your own self and give love to others and respect your own values. "Be grateful to everyone, because everybody is creating a space for you to be transformed – even those who think they are obstructing you, even those whom you think are enemies. Your friends, your enemies, good people and bad people, favorable circumstances, unfavorable circumstances – all together they are creating the context in which you can be transformed and become a Buddha. Be grateful to all. To those who have helped, to those who have hindered, to those who have been indifferent. Be grateful to all, because all together they are creating the context in which Buddhas are born, in which you can become a Buddha."

I think its time for me to conclude, I have always longed to write a book, but because of my laziness I kept on posting it for tomorrow, where tomorrow never happened in all these years, the reason is I don't know what my interests are and what would make me happy, so all these years I kept on fluctuating, because I couldn't find any satisfaction in what I did, I lost happiness. I might have had hints within in my life to follow life according to my happiness, which at times the environment which I lived in differed, and my life has been diverted to a different direction. But from the beginning love has been involved in life, since I never knew or realized what love was I never took my life very seriously, as years passed I myself had a question about life which made me think, I think somewhere within there was a master who always tried to help me in my life, which I never recognized; though I had a vision of a great mystic master I failed to recognize, but somewhere within an unknown master was pushing me to the real world to experience and to observe what is happening in and out. It's a busy world out there, you don't recognize it, you don't observe, you don't remember because life has no time, we say a miracle happens for a very few, no not at all, miracles happen to everyone. How many of us recognize and realize it and implement this in our life? Vision is not rare, it is frequent, how many of us remember, in my case I recognized that very moment in my life because of my father, else I would not even have recognized; though I had a vision, I never had any news or any new teachings about spirituality or about God by the Bhagvan, it was just like a casual visit or it was just like an accident that I happened to see him like I saw others in my life. Though I felt that I was not able to recognize him, I have never felt bad, because I grew up like all others in this modern world, without knowing what spirituality is, so I never read or never knew any spiritual leaders in India. So it was totally my mistake and I blame myself for that mistake because I was not able to recognize who the master is. I will not say that vision which I had was a miracle, but the change which I had within, when I had a chance to recognize the master through his inspiration, the sudden change in my attitude about life and love totally changed, which is what I would say "miracle." He made me realize what life and love are, no one has advised me to do meditation, to become involved in spirituality, all these were not my idea either, but the change within made me love, pushed me within an inner world of love, to experience love within which made realize the outer world concepts about life and love, which is what the book is all about. This book is not to hurt others views on love, this is my experience, self experience within, I personally apologize if I have hurt others' opinion on love, each one's experience and thoughts may differ, but the concept is the same, which is what I am trying to convey, my life's experience and observation about love is what I have tried to explain. I am not encouraging or motivating or forcing someone to follow, you look at the mirror and you see your own self in it, likewise my experience is something similar, you may or may not see yourself when you read, if you see your own self, then that's my success. When I started to write, I had no idea about publishing, I just expressed myself because when I started writing I felt immense joy within, which I never felt before in any other profession. I don't how my future is going, I don't expect, I just leave it to life, no one will face it for you, you are the only one to face it with full courage, which is what most of us lack within. If you can experience the fear in you with joy you can experience your true self; I am not a master here to advise, I still don't know anything about this, I am still learning, experiencing it and observing it within, this is just a journey which I am experiencing to know my unknown master within, it may even take my lifetime to understand and observe the unknown. Everyone of us has been taught in such a way that God is a character, God and love is not a character or an object to be grabbed or bought, it is an invisible energy a power within, from the ancient time this is what has been followed, when population and technology increased, humans' mentalities have been totally changed, ancient history says that there was no poverty and unemployment, but that's not what our modern world is now. So spirituality in those times was totally different and now spirituality is something different, spirituality may change from time to time but love in spirituality will never change, it remains the same, which is what I am pointing out here, spirituality forms within when love forms, meditation is a possibility, to make meditation possible you need to understand what meditation is or else you can follow life with an understanding in love, for that love you should start loving your own self and then think about sharing it with others, forget false love and follow pure love. Meditation is not the only source to be spiritual; it is a factor to experience the unknown within. There are people who do meditation without even knowing why they do that, the truth is what did you experience out of it and how far did you implement those facts in reality? The world is full of entertainment, but there is no celebration, in ancient times there seems to be a lot of celebration because there was no entertainment, but the modern world lacked celebration, it has been locked with entertainment, how can we celebrate each and every moment, celebrate with the outer world, celebrate love within? The whole concept of love is to celebrate, as I said people change accordingly so celebration also changes.

This book is not fiction, thriller or a novel, it is just an experience about life within, every book has a climax section where the story either ends happily or ends with a sad note, since this book is my life I don't know what happens next because this is not my end, this is just my beginning, this book talks about different views on love, which includes my personal experiences and other great masters' views as well as my personal opinion. Never judge a person by his or her physical experience, likewise never judge a book without reading it completely, it's up to you whether to follow or not, if my experience acts as a mirror at least for an individual, if he feels so then that is where my success lies, I have not mentioned any characters by giving a name to them, the reason I never gave a name is I personally felt that I shouldn't hurt or play with others' emotions which is not healthy. The incidents which I have mentioned in this book are all my personal observations about my life and about love with the help of the master within who is UNKNOWN ... let everyone be blessed with the showering of love in life and let everyone live happily lifelong realizing the truth about love, which is already within, and with just a little effort wake the master within who is always with you. "Understanding cannot be studied; nobody can teach it to you. You have to be a light unto yourself. You have to seek and search within your own being, because it is already there at the very core. If you dive deep you will find it. You will have to learn how to dive within yourself – not in the scriptures, but within your own existence."